IR

THE RIDESHARE GUIDE

D0029248

THE RIDESHARE GUIDE

EVERYTHING YOU NEED TO KNOW ABOUT DRIVING FOR UBER, LYFT, AND OTHER RIDESHARING COMPANIES

HARRY CAMPBELL

Skyhorse Publishing

Skyhorse Publishing books may be purchased in bulk at special discounts for sales promotion, corporate gifts, fund-raising, or educational purposes. Special editions can also be created to specifications. For details, contact the Special Sales Department, Skyhorse Publishing, 307 West 36th Street, 11th Floor, New York, NY 10018 or info@skyhorsepublishing.com.

Skyhorse® and Skyhorse Publishing® are registered trademarks of Skyhorse Publishing, Inc.®, a Delaware corporation.

Visit our website at www.skyhorsepublishing.com.

10 9 8 7 6 5 4 3 2 1

Library of Congress Cataloging-in-Publication Data is available on file.

Cover design by Rain Saukas

Cover photo credit Harry Campbell

ISBN: 978-1-5107-3531-6
Ebook ISBN: 978-1-5107-3532-3

Printed in the United States of America

Table of Contents

Acknowledgments

I'd like to thank my readers and fans for their support over the years. I don't know that I've made a huge impact on their lives but I've enjoyed running a profitable business that is based on helping others. My hope is that this book inspires others to do more of the same.

And thanks to my wife (who will probably never read this book), my newborn son, my team at The Rideshare Guy, and Skyhorse Publishing. They all work together to help me look better than I actually am.

—Harry

Introduction
Why drive for Uber or Lyft?

IT WASN'T THAT LONG AGO that Uber and Lyft were niche rideshare services for techies in San Francisco, and the thought of hitching a ride with a stranger was completely foreign. But once passengers got a taste of hailing rides from their smartphones, paying with a credit card, and rating their driver, they were hooked! The stark contrast of rideshare from the more traditional taxi experience turned average consumers into raving fans. Best of all, these rides were way cheaper than a taxi.

Over the past few years, Uber and its main competitor, Lyft, have exploded onto the scene. Lyft focuses on the United States while Uber is in hundreds of cities worldwide, but both services are still growing rapidly. According to a Pew Research study in 2016,[1] over half of all Americans

1   http://www.pewinternet.org/2016/05/19/on-demand-ride-hailing-apps/.

have already heard of Uber and the company is now expanding into other verticals like food delivery, packages, and even UberAir.

But buried beneath all the flashy technology and explosive growth is an army of drivers who keeps these services moving. Uber currently has over two million drivers[2] while Lyft has nearly seven hundred thousand more.[3] The rapid growth has created a ton of employment opportunities, but there's also a void in training and information because the industry is so new. Nobody grew up thinking they'd be an Uber driver someday because the company didn't even exist a decade ago! I'll help fill that void with this book.

Whenever I talk to drivers about why they work for Uber, two themes consistently come up. The first thing that drivers care about is pay because, well, everyone cares about how much they get paid, right? After pay, drivers care deeply about the flexibility that comes with driving for Uber and Lyft, and that's what makes this job so unique.

I've worked all sorts of jobs in my life but it wasn't until I started driving with Uber and Lyft that I got my first sign-up bonus for starting a new job. Sign-up bonuses can vary by city but usually the bigger the city, the higher the bonus. Both Uber and Lyft routinely offer bonuses (or guaranteed earnings) of hundreds of dollars in major cities like New York, Los Angeles, and San Francisco and if you're a new driver, it's something that we'll teach you how to take advantage of in chapter 1.

---

2   https://www.thebillfold.com/2017/08/uber-drivers-have-earned-50-million-in-tips-but-there-are-2-million-drivers/.

3   https://www.cnbc.com/2017/03/17/judge-approves-27-million-driver-settlement-in-lyft-lawsuit.html/

Unlike other jobs, as a rideshare driver you'll see a direct correlation between how hard you work and how much money you make. If you wake up one day and realize you need to drive twelve hours to pay off a bill, you can do just that. But while you can always work more hours, a lot of the strategies and topics we cover in this book will help you work smarter, not harder. In fact, there are a whole host of applications, tools, and strategies that you will be able to apply that will help you outearn your fellow driver.

Most outsiders don't realize how flexible working for Uber can be. Uber uses marketing slogans like "Be Your Own Boss" and "The Ultimate Side Hustle" and for the most part, those sayings are true. There's no set schedule with Uber or Lyft, so whenever you want to drive, all you have to do is log on to the app and work for as long or as short as you want.

Drivers can also set destinations in order to get rides only headed in a specific direction, making it feasible to do a couple Uber rides on your way to work every morning. If your boss is strict, you can even set an arrival time to guarantee that you'll be at your final destination on time. Lyft has a similar feature called Driver Destinations; the competition between the two rideshare giants often means that these companies are constantly fighting over drivers and appropriating each other's best ideas.

This flexibility makes it desirable for a lot of people and frankly, I can't think of another job that comes even close in this department for both time and money. In 2016, Uber launched a new feature called Instant Pay that allows drivers to instantly cash out their earnings to their bank account as often as they'd like for a nominal fee. Lyft has a similar feature called Express Pay.

Being your own boss is great since you can work whenever you want and as much or as little as you want, but it also means that you're responsible for things like expenses, tracking your mileage, diversifying your income sources, getting adequate rideshare insurance, and thinking about potential liability issues. While that may sound like a lot of work, this guide will help you with everything you need for the journey.

I've been driving for Uber and Lyft since 2014 (which makes me really old in rideshare years!) but I've learned a ton about what it takes to be successful at this gig and how to make it worthwhile. In this book, you'll learn exactly what you need to get started and I will share all the tips, tricks, and secrets of the trade to help you earn more while on the road.

I won't ever tell you that you should or shouldn't do this job, but I am going to present the facts—facts based off real-life driving experience and facts based off tens of thousands of interactions with real-life drivers. I've heard it all when it comes to being an Uber or Lyft driver, and I firmly believe that anyone who is motivated to learn this new industry and new line of work will be successful.

So if you're ready, let's hit the road!

1
What's it really like to be a rideshare driver?

I STILL REMEMBER MY FIRST ride as an Uber passenger all the way back in 2013. My driver was telling me about all the fun drunks he was picking up and, most importantly, how he was making a ton of money for a job that was actually pretty fun. That first driver I took a ride with had nothing but good things to say about the company and since my real job at the time had me working all day in a cubicle, getting paid to drive people around and talk to them sounded like a no-brainer.

Now, a lot of you might be wondering *How hard could it be to drive for Uber?* To be fair, that's usually the first question people ask when I tell them I run a blog that helps Uber and Lyft drivers. My answer to that question is simple: Being an Uber driver isn't rocket science, but it is a little harder than it looks. While most of us know how to drive a car, once you start to involve other people, a ratings system, and alcohol, things get a bit more challenging. Driving for hire is the ultimate combination of customer service, safe driving, navigation, and strategy.

Even though it may be fun to hype up the life of a rideshare driver, it's not all glitz and glamour. Uber has over two million drivers on their platform, but half of them will end up quitting after just one year.[4] High turnover means that there are a lot of obstacles to overcome but if you can figure it out, being a rideshare driver could prove to be one of the most unique work experiences in your lifetime.

How much you'll make as a rideshare driver

Driving for Uber or Lyft has its perks but at the end of the day, it's not something I would ever do for free! The average driver reports[5] earning around $16–18 per hour before expenses, but a lot of variability is behind those numbers.

Unlike a cashier job where everyone gets paid the same amount from day one, different drivers will end up with different earnings. The amount you make will depend heavily on when and where you drive. Driving in busy cities like San Francisco, Los Angeles, and Chicago is more lucrative than driving in smaller or mid-tier cities since there's so much more demand. Now, you might not be able to control where you live, but as many drivers discover, it pays to drive in the busiest places.

---

4   https://s3.amazonaws.com/uber-static/comms/PDF/Uber_Driver-Partners_Hall_Kreuger_2015.pdf.
5   https:// therideshareguy.com/rsg-2017-survey-results-driver-earnings-satisfaction-and-demographics/.

As an Uber or Lyft driver, you'll also want to consider when you plan on driving. Uber offers a ton of flexibility but in order to maximize your profits, you'll want to focus on the busiest times to drive. Typically, the peak hours occur during weekday commuting hours and Friday and Saturday nights. Now, you don't have to drive during those times to make money but that's usually when it's the busiest and you'll be able to maximize your profits. (See chapter 5 for more info on maximizing your profits.)

I drive part-time in Los Angeles but I hate traffic. I've always targeted the weekends and after traffic dies down on the weekdays, which can be very profitable. So even though the average driver reports making $16–18 per hour, I usually aim for $20–$30 per hour. Here's what a recent weekend of driving looked like for me:[6]

	# of rides	Hours Worked	Gross Pay	Gross Pay per Hour	Total Miles Driven
Wednesday	8	3:08:00	$54.60	$17.43	80.9
Thursday	10	3:57:00	$63.94	$16.19	94.7
Friday	12	4:02:00	$78.67	$19.50	76.5
Saturday	22	7:54:00	$261.97	$33.16	213.9
Total/Average	52	19:01:00	$459.18	$24.15	466

Table 1: *Earnings for a week of driving in Los Angeles, CA - March 2017*

As you can see, I hit my goal of $20–$30 per hour but there was a lot of variability from Wednesday to Saturday. I

6   http://therideshareguy.com/how-much-money-can-an-uber-and-lyft-driver-make-in-2017/.

averaged only $16–$17 per hour on the weekday nights but on Saturday, my average hourly earnings jumped up to $33 per hour.

You probably won't hit these numbers from the get-go, but it should be used as a gauge for the potential earnings as a driver. I hear from drivers all the time who are struggling to make minimum wage, but that's because they're not doing everything they can to maximize their earnings.

Remember, there's no minimum wage as a rideshare driver and there are no guarantees when it comes to how much money you can make driving for Uber and Lyft. But the smarter you work and the more strategy that you employ, the higher your earnings can rise.

As a driver for rideshare services, you're actually a 1099 independent contractor, which means you'll be responsible for all of your expenses, and come tax time you will need to file a Schedule C. Don't let that scare you, since I'll make sure you have everything you need to stay ahead of the game in regards to taxes and reporting. Chapter 8 will go over rideshare taxes and show you exactly what you'll need to do come tax time.

What your expenses will look like

Rideshare drivers will put a lot of miles on their cars. A full-time driver can easily do a thousand miles a week or more and if you refer back to table 1, you'll notice that the last column shows that I drove 466 miles in order to earn my $459.18. So if your car gets 25 miles per gallon and gas costs $3 per gallon, you'll have to subtract the cost of gas from your earnings.

(466 miles / 25 miles per gallon) x \$3 per gallon = \$55.92
(my total fuel cost for a weekend of driving)

If we subtract the total fuel cost of \$55.92 from my gross earnings of \$459.18, my net earnings come out to \$403.26. So now you know why so many Prius drivers are on Uber and Lyft! The cost of fuel cuts into your earnings and that's why it's so important to have a car that gets great mileage, especially if you're going to be a full-time driver. We'll cover the full cost of operating your vehicle in chapter 8 but in short, you get paid the same whether you drive a gas guzzling SUV or a fuel-efficient hybrid. So the car you drive can have a big impact on your bottom line.

Why Uber and Lyft are the most flexible jobs in the world

Let's say you need to make \$50 for an upcoming bill or even a night out on the town. With Uber or Lyft, you can flip on your app and work a few hours until you hit \$50, cash out that money instantly, and not work again until you need to do the same thing over again.

There aren't many jobs with this type of scheduling flexibility, and if you're anything like me, having the ability to make money on a whim could really come in handy.

> Jay Cradeur got the inspiration to drive from his daughter, a millennial! She enjoyed driving for Uber, and Jay, wanting flexibility so he could keep up his passion for travel, tried driving in 2015. He made \$100 in his first six hours driving and was hooked!

Jay started off driving in the Sacramento market but he soon relocated to San Francisco to take advantage of all the driving opportunities in that city and now drives full-time. The extra money he makes as a full-time driver with all the bonuses has made a big difference in his income, and the weekly incentives and bonuses accounted for 25 percent of his revenue in 2016.

His full-time rideshare driving job pays for all of his bills, helps to support his daughter in college, and enables him to travel. In 2017, he took three-week vacations—even to exotic locations like Bali!

You can learn more about Jay here: therideshareguy.com/JayCradeur

Even though Uber provides the ultimate flexibility, most people don't need it. You probably won't want to sign on to the Uber app and do one ride and then turn it off because that isn't very efficient. Most drivers work in blocks of three to four hours or more. And since the average ride is around ten to fifteen minutes, you'll want to work enough to get in a rhythm and start earning decent money.

Uber and Lyft don't set maximum hours that you can work[7] but it's important that you stay safe on the road. I generally try and take a break every couple hours, even if it's just to use the bathroom or stretch. Sitting in a car for hours on end can be detrimental to your health so it's important

---

7   Some cities like Chicago and New York have restrictions on the number of consecutive hours that a driver can work for one platform.

that you stay hydrated and move around when you can. We'll expand on this topic in chapter 8.

Getting your Uber and Lyft sign-up bonuses!

Uber and Lyft have raised billions of dollars from investors over the years, and a lot of that money goes into subsidies for drivers and passengers. We'll learn more about the weekly bonus and incentive programs that Uber and Lyft offer in chapter 5, but one of the first things you'll want to take advantage of as you start off is the potential sign-up bonus for new drivers.

Uber and Lyft offer sign-up bonuses to brand-new drivers that can range from $25–$50 all the way up to $500 in bigger cities. Typically, the more demand there is for drivers, the higher the bonus that the companies will offer.

But as you can imagine, there are a couple hoops to jump through in order to get such a big bonus. Neither company publishes a list of sign-up bonuses online, but try and reach out to the company directly to find out what they're currently offering. You can always sign up to drive directly on the Uber or Lyft website, but I don't recommend it since then you won't be eligible for a sign-up bonus. If you want to get a bonus, you'll need to make sure you go through an existing driver's referral link.

If you haven't signed up yet and you'd like to use my information, I've included my referral codes and direct sign up links below:

- Uber: Use code **3e3dg** or direct link:
  www.therideshareguy.com/newuberdriver

- Lyft: Use code **Harry757** or direct link: www.therideshareguy.com/newlyftdriver

Sometimes, drivers sign up with Uber but forget to enter a referral code. In this instance, Uber gives you ten to fifteen days from when you're activated as a driver to submit a retroactive referral code. You can reference my website for the latest instructions on this process: www.therideshareguy.com/sign-up-bonuses.

Lyft does not allow for drivers to retroactively submit a referral code so make sure that you enter it correctly the first time around.

If you're wondering when the best time is to sign up for Uber or Lyft and take advantage of sign-up bonuses, demand for drivers usually spikes in the early summer and at the end of the year since Halloween, Thanksgiving Eve, and New Year's Eve are a few of the biggest driving nights of the year. So, if you can take advantage of a bonus to get started, great, but don't let that hold you back.

In 2017, Uber started rolling out a new bonus program for new drivers called "Guaranteed Earnings." Guaranteed earnings have now replaced sign-up bonuses in most markets and the way this program works is slightly different.

You'll still need to use a referral link of an existing driver to be eligible, but instead of a bonus, Uber guarantees new drivers that they will earn a certain amount after a specific number of trips.

Please note that the amounts and details listed in table 2 change continuously and may no longer be applicable by the time you are reading this book, but they should give you an idea of how the program works and how the amounts vary by city. In San Francisco for example, drivers

City	Invitee Guarantee	Trip Requirement	$/trip
San Francisco	$1,000	100	$10.00
Chicago	$520	75	$6.93
San Diego	$520	75	$6.93
Orange County	$490	75	$6.53
Los Angeles	$470	75	$6.27
Denver	$400	50	$8.00
Boston	$380	50	$7.60
Washington D.C.	$370	50	$7.40
Dallas	$350	50	$7.00
Miami	$320	50	$6.40

Table 2: Guaranteed Earnings for New Uber Drivers by City - June 2017

were guaranteed, under this promotion, $1,000 in earnings within their first one hundred trips, or $10/trip. Based off data we've collected, the average trip payout to a driver is around $7, so if you earn $700 under this program, Uber would pay you an additional $300.

To maximize your earnings on the guaranteed system, you'll want to complete as many short rides as possible. This is the opposite of a typical driving strategy, as medium to longer rides mean bigger fares. But if your earnings are guaranteed, you'll improve your profit margin by completing lots of short trips and cashing out on the guarantee.

This is easier said than done, of course, but there are a few tricks you can use. Avoid early morning trips to the airport (and the airport itself). Instead, focus on the busy evening hours when trip requests are frequent and short. You'll get plenty of folks hopping around between local restaurants or bars, which means plenty of minimum-fare rides.

By completing lots of short trips, you'll minimize the gas, maintenance, and time expenditures needed to meet the ride requirement, and you'll be more likely to receive extra money on top of what you made in fares, which will increase your overall profit margin. We'll go more into the best driving strategies in chapter 5, but this should give you a taste of what to expect.

Uber and Lyft driver requirements

Sometimes I like to joke that if you have a pulse and can pass a background check, you can drive for Uber or Lyft. For a lot of drivers, this is a good thing since Uber and Lyft do not discriminate whatsoever based on age, race, or sex. So as long as you can meet all the requirements, they're happy to have you.

There are no costs or fees to apply, but you do have to apply online and go through a standard online background check. In order to be eligible, you must meet the following criteria:

- You must be twenty-one years of age or older AND have three years of US driving experience. Or you can be twenty-three years of age or older with one or more years of US driving experience.
- You must have an in-state driver's license in order to drive with Uber.

- You must have in-state personal auto insurance AND your name must be listed on the insurance card.
- Your car needs to be registered in-state but your name does not have to be on the registration.

If you meet all of the above criteria, the next step is to pass an online background check. A Social Security number is needed to process it. The background check will look at the following and goes back seven years:

- You will need a clean driving record.
- No DUI or drug-related offenses.
- No history of reckless driving.
- No fatal accidents.
- No criminal record.

Pro-tip: The company that processes the background checks for Uber is called Checkr. If you have any problems with your background check, email them at support@checkr.com. Be sure to include your name, phone number, and email address in the body of the email. You can also contact Checkr at 844-824-3257. Lyft uses Sterling Talent Solutions for their background checks and you can contact Lyft on help.lyft.com if you need to inquire about the status of your application.

Once you pass the background check, you'll need a smartphone and an eligible vehicle. Any smartphone will do, but since you often run multiple apps at once (Uber, Lyft, GPS/Navigation, etc), a latest or second-generation phone is your best bet.

Some cities have special car requirements, but for the most part, you can drive for Uber with a 2002 or newer vehicle—in cities like Los Angeles, San Francisco, and Chicago—that is in good running condition; this means no large dents, damage, or chipped paint.

Here's a list of all the UberX vehicle requirements:

- Four-door sedan; must have five total seat belts.
- Year 2002* or newer in most cities.
- In-state license plates.
- No marked, taxi, or salvaged vehicles.
- Pass the Uber vehicle inspection.
- Registration must be up to date, but your name does not have to be on the registration.

*Check help.uber.com and enter your city to get the specific vehicle year requirements for your area.

Ninety percent of Uber's business happens on UberX but if you've got a nicer, bigger, or more luxurious car, Uber does have other levels of service. We'll expand on all the different options in chapter 2.

Lyft requires all vehicles to be 2005 or newer, although there are some exceptions and you can find the latest info on Lyft's website.[8] For the most part, both companies have pretty much the same requirements regarding background checks and vehicles.

---

8   https://help.lyft.com/hc/en-us/articles/214219557-Vehicle -requirements.

Leasing or renting rideshare vehicles

One of the major requirements holding back a lot of drivers is an eligible vehicle. If you're interested in driving for Uber or Lyft but don't have an eligible car, you still have a few options for getting on the road.

Since rideshare drivers put so many miles on their car, a normal lease usually won't make a lot of sense for a potential Uber or Lyft driver. Instead, you'll want to find a rideshare-specific lease or rental program.

Uber Xchange Leasing was one of the most popular options but they stopped accepting new applications in 2017. Lyft has a similar program called Lyft Express Drive that has been very popular and it allows drivers to rent a vehicle for anywhere from $185–$235 per week. This is obviously much more expensive than a traditional lease or car payment, but it's also more flexible and comes with unlimited mileage and free maintenance.

HyreCar is a third-party option that allows private owners to rent out their cars on a weekly or even daily basis to rideshare drivers. One of the nice things about going this route is that you are eligible to drive for both Uber and Lyft.

For a full list of all the latest vehicle leasing and rental programs, please check: therideshareguy.com/Vehicles.

The downsides of being a rideshare driver

Let me start this section by telling you that this job is not for everyone. I've always driven for Uber and Lyft part-time since I feel that that's the best way to maximize the experience. Rideshare offers drivers the ultimate flexibility but if you have to drive forty or fifty hours a week, you won't be able to take advantage of the flexibility nearly as much. That being said, for a lot of people who need flexible work arrangements or are out of work, doing Uber and Lyft full-time can be a lifesaver.

Rideshare pay can range from $5–$10 per hour on weekday afternoons to $20–$30 or more per hour on Friday and Saturday nights. So there are only a certain number of highly profitable hours that you can target every week, and for the most part, the more you drive, the lower your average hourly pay will likely fall (unless your city has weekly bonus offers as we'll learn about in chapter 5).

If you look at the history of Uber though, the company was founded by entrepreneurs who were looking for a better way to call for a ride, not with taxi drivers who were fed up with the system. So one of the biggest complaints I hear from drivers is that the company can be too passenger-centric at times. Uber is starting to value drivers more but a lot of the issues drivers face these days stem from this initial passenger-centric focus.

I'm biased but I fundamentally believe that drivers are key to the success of these platforms going forward. Uber has always acknowledged that they have problems with high turnover and low satisfaction rates among drivers, but it wasn't until 2017 that the company really started to do something about it. That's when they announced a new initiative called "180 Days of Change," and the first thing they did was add a tipping option to the Uber app. This had long been a point of frustration for Uber drivers and it appears to be a turning point in the company's relationship with its drivers.

Lyft has always had a better relationship with drivers and this stems from a more playful initial culture that encouraged passengers to sit up front, fist bump their driver, and leave a tip. The Lyft experience has become more homogenous over the years, but both companies appear to be changing and adapting for the better.

Since the industry is so new, these companies are very young and with immaturity comes growing pains. The most important piece of advice that I can give you is that in order to be successful as an Uber or Lyft driver, you're going to need to think like a business owner. Because, whether you realize it or not, drivers are paid as 1099 contractors, and as soon as you hit the road, you've got a business!

2
How do I get started as a driver?

So NOW YOU KNOW WHAT the realities of rideshare driving are, and you've decided you're ready to sign up and get started. I've been there. In fact, I still remember the Newport Beach apartment I lived in when I first signed up to drive with Uber and Lyft. I filled out the applications from my couch and within a few days I was approved to drive.

One of the best parts about signing up to drive with Uber and Lyft is that there aren't a ton of requirements. Uber will basically take anyone as long as you can pass a background check and have a car and a smartphone. So, most people won't need to make a big investment of time or money in order to try this job out. And as we'll read about in chapter 10, this goes both ways since driver saturation also means that the more drivers there are, the more competition there will be for those rides.

But when you're first getting started as a driver, all that really matters is whether or not you can get hired. Uber and Lyft make this part easy and many drivers who have struggled to get hired in other industries are pleasantly surprised to find that Uber does not care about age, gender, or ethnicity.

Rob Saunders had recently retired from the corporate world at the tender age of 55 and was looking for a way to supplement his income. He wasn't yet 59 ½, so he couldn't touch his retirement without penalty, and he was struggling to find the right part-time job. It can be pretty tough for baby boomers to find part-time jobs, as some employers may make the assumption that older workers can't be taught new things.

One day, Rob stumbled upon Uber and Lyft and decided to give it a try for a couple reasons: (1) flexibility, (2) rideshare driving is for people of all ages. According to Rob, there's no age discrimination when you're your own boss.

Overall, baby boomers can make great drivers and shouldn't be intimidated by the technology. As Rob says, baby boomers have been learning new tech skills since they were kids, and rideshare driving with apps is just one new skill to learn.

Listen to our interview with Rob Saunders at therideshareguy.com/episode17.

Choosing Uber or Lyft to start

Although Uber was founded all the way back in 2009,[9] it was actually Lyft (and Sidecar before them) that pioneered the ridesharing model we all know and love today. Uber initially focused on the existing commercial black car market while Lyft tried to get regular people like you and me to pick up strangers for money.

Both companies were based out of San Francisco, and while Lyft dominated the city's skyline with its pink mustaches and fist bumps for the first couple years, it wasn't long before Uber copied that model and launched UberX, which is their most popular service today.

Uber has dominated the market ever since, and while the company doesn't show any signs of slowing down, Lyft is still a formidable opponent. Here's a quick comparison of how the two companies stack up:

- Uber is in over six hundred cities worldwide, while Lyft operates in three hundred US Cities but has recently started expanding internationally.
- Uber has two million drivers worldwide while Lyft has seven hundred thousand drivers in the United States.
- Today, Uber has around 75 percent market share in the United States while Lyft retains a respectable 25 percent market share.[10]
- Uber has been privately valued at over $69 billion and raised $12 billion in cash.[11]

---

9   https://en.wikipedia.org/wiki/Uber_(company).

10   https://www.usatoday.com/story/tech/news/2017/06/13/uber-market-share-customer-image-hit-string-scandals/102795024/.

11   https://www.recode.net/2017/5/25/15686886/ride-hail-valuation-investment-uber-didi-lyft.

- Lyft has been privately valued at $11 billion and has raised over $3.6 billion in cash.[12]

At the core of both companies, they do basically the same thing: Uber and Lyft connect drivers with riders to get you safely from point A to point B. If you're thinking that sounds like a taxi, you're right!

Uber and Lyft are basically glorified taxi apps, but they do have some built-in features that make the product vastly superior to taxis. Riders love the ability to hail a ride with a smartphone, pay with credit card, and rate their driver. And drivers love the flexibility of using their own car and working whenever and wherever they want.

But if we go beyond the numbers and look at what each company stands for, that will tell us a lot about each company's culture and where the differences lie.

If you remember, Uber was founded by guys who wanted a better way of calling for a ride, so these were not founders who wanted to improve the taxi driver experience. They were much more focused on improving the passenger experience and that passenger-centric culture has continued to this day.

Uber's initial company slogan was "Everyone's private driver," and since Uber primarily catered to higher-end black car clients at the start, a lot of that branding plays out in their products. Uber started with luxury vehicles and catered to high-end clients before branching out to UberX. As a driver, I've always noticed that Uber passengers seem to keep you waiting longer and not be as respectful as Lyft passengers. So at times, it can feel like Uber has more of the

---

12   https://www.recode.net/2017/10/19/16503628/alphabet-lyft-ride-hail-investment-billion.

corporate feel with you working for your passengers while Lyft has always had more of a community feel.

At its onset, Lyft encouraged drivers to sport a pink mustache on the hood and to fist bump passengers when they got into the car. Most riders sat up front and the company has always had a more driver-centric focus. They were the first to launch features like in app tipping; in-person meetups for drivers; and the Power Driver Bonus, which gave drivers some or all of their commission back for hitting weekly ride goals.

Times have changed since those early days and the relationship between driver and rider has become more transactional in nature. Even so, I've always felt that most drivers prefer working for Lyft but they get more rides and make more money with Uber.

In a recent survey[13] of over 1,100 drivers on

---

13   http://therideshareguy.com/rsg-2017-survey-results-driver-earnings-satisfaction-and-demographics/.

TheRideshareGuy.com, 75.8 percent of drivers reported that they were satisfied with their experience driving for Lyft, while just 49.4 percent of drivers reported that they were satisfied with their experience driving for Uber.

Overall, I am satisfied with my experience driving for LYFT.

235 responses

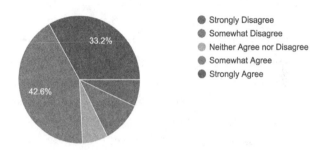

- Strongly Disagree
- Somewhat Disagree
- Neither Agree nor Disagree
- Somewhat Agree
- Strongly Agree

Overall, I am satisfied with my experience driving for UBER.

863 responses

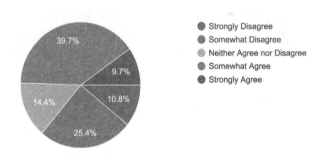

- Strongly Disagree
- Somewhat Disagree
- Neither Agree nor Disagree
- Somewhat Agree
- Strongly Agree

Lyft may seem like the more driver-friendly choice, but ultimately you're going to want to sign up for both apps anyway. As we'll learn in chapter 5, drivers are independent contractors, which means you can and should work for multiple services. Uber and Lyft probably won't tell you to sign up for their competitor, but I will!

When you're just getting started though, pick one company and learn the ropes with them first before signing up for the other. If you're looking for the more businesslike vibe, Uber will be right up your alley; if you prefer a more laid-back community feel, Lyft may be the better choice.

Radio personality and consumer expert Clark Howard was challenged by one of his readers to try out driving for Uber and Lyft and he ended up doing just that. Clark signed up for both companies and at first, he was making only around $12 an hour, but that was as a completely new driver with no real understanding of surge or even placement. As Clark learned the ropes, he found that just by driving a few minutes into the city was the difference between no fares at all and fare after fare.

Clark's experiment shows that it pays to be aware of surge pricing, where the hot spots are in your city, and how setting yourself up to drive for the day/night is very important. Although Clark is back to his nationally syndicated radio show, he still sees driving for rideshare as a good way to make supplemental income.

All the different levels of Uber (UberX, UberPOOL, UberXL, UberSelect)

One of the most confusing parts about signing up to drive with Uber is figuring out which level of service your car is eligible for. Most likely, you'll fall under UberX, which is their standard service and typically consists of basic four-door sedans like a Toyota Prius, Ford Fusion, or Chevy Cruze.

Uber has a few different levels of service that you may be eligible for depending on the type of vehicle you drive. Not every city will have all of these options but the bigger your city is, the better the odds that all of these options will be available.

Here's a brief overview of each level of service:

UberX: UberX makes up 90 percent of the rides on the Uber platform and typically these rides will be served by four-door sedans that can carry at least four passengers with seat belts (in addition to the driver).

UberPOOL: UberPOOL is a carpooling service that matches groups of one or two riders headed in the same direction. As an UberX driver, you may also be sent UberPOOL requests at any time.

UberSELECT: UberSELECT is Uber's mid-level luxury service with rates two to three times higher than UberX. In order to be eligible, you'll need a newer luxury vehicle, like a Lexus or BMW.

UberXL: UberXL is Uber's high-capacity option, and vehicles are required to be able to carry at least six passengers in addition to the driver. Think minivans and three-row SUVs.

Drivers may be eligible for more than one level of service, but you can never go up in service. So if you're an UberX driver, you won't be able to do UberSELECT or UberXL unless you get a nicer or bigger car.

UberXL and UberSELECT drivers, on the other hand, can accept UberX and UberPOOL requests. If your car is eligible, you'll be able to set trip preferences under the settings menu on the driver app so that you have the option of getting UberSELECT-only rides or UberSELECT and UberX, as we'll discuss in chapter 4.

If you remember, Uber started off as a black car–only service and they still have those levels of service, but they're what's known as Uber's commercial platforms since the requirements are much stricter. Drivers for UberBLACK and UberSUV must have commercial insurance and taxi licensing. We'll go into more detail about how to drive UberBLACK in chapter 9.

Lyft offers an array of similar services with different names, but the requirements are pretty similar. Here's how they stack up to Uber's comparable services.

Lyft = UberX
Line = UberPOOL
Premier = UberSELECT
Plus = UberXL
Lux = UberBLACK
Lux SUV = UberSUV

My advice is to start with UberX or Lyft until you know the ropes. When you're ready, more info on the other services can be found in chapter 9.

UberX in New York City

It's important to talk about New York City (NYC) for a minute since it's the largest transportation market in the world, but it's also the only place in the United States where UberX drivers have to maintain commercial insurance and be licensed by the NYC Taxi & Limousine Commission (TLC).

The rates in NYC are higher to reflect the additional costs, but it also means that it doesn't make a lot of sense to be a part-time driver there since you have such high costs. Many drivers end up working through a fleet owner where they pay a weekly rental fee for a car that's already registered to drive with Uber, and the owner covers maintenance, licensing, and fees while the driver is only responsible for the weekly rental fee and gas.

You can still drive for competitors like Lyft, Juno, and Via but you'll find that the NYC UberX experience is pretty atypical compared to every other city in the United States.

The first two products you'll need to buy as a rideshare driver

Although you don't need anything other than a smartphone and an eligible vehicle to drive with Uber, there are a few products that I highly recommend to new drivers. Since Uber and Lyft can't provide equipment due to the independent contractor nature of their relationship with drivers, you'll be responsible for providing all equipment. But as we'll read about in chapter 8, all of the products you purchase for your business should be tax deductible.

The first product that I always recommend to new drivers is a phone mount. Unsafe driving and poor navigation is the number one reason that riders leave low ratings, and if you're constantly staring at your lap, your eyes won't be on the road.

There are a number of phone mounts that you can purchase, but we've found that those with magnetized backings

The Kenu Airframe easily attaches to any vent in your car.

are great for pulling your phone on or off of the mount. Scosche is a top brand for magnetic mounts; other drivers prefer air vent mounts like the Kenu Airframe.

You can find a full review of several different options on the blog: www.therideshareguy.com/phonemounts.

Once you've picked out a mount, make sure your phone is mounted within your peripheral vision as you drive so when you switch your focus toward it, the road is still visible. Phone mounts are relatively inexpensive (in the $10–30 range) so there's no excuse for not having one.

Another popular item that more and more drivers are starting to purchase is a dash cam. A wide variety of dash cams are the market, but the main reason to have one is for your personal safety and liability. Since many drivers work during Friday and Saturday nights, you will encounter your fair share of intoxicated passengers, and although I've never had anything go really wrong in my car, it's good to have a dash cam recording just in case.

I've also found that when passengers know they're on camera, they tend to be better behaved. You will want to make sure you follow all local/state laws when recording

The Falcon Dashcam attaches to your existing mirror and has a forward and rear facing camera.

passengers. Here in California, for example, I have to put a sticker on my window to let passengers know that audio and video are being recorded. These stickers can be purchased on Amazon.com for a nominal price.

Still not convinced? Even if you think you're the best driver in the world, another driver could hit you, costing you thousands in repairs, potential medical bills, and putting you out of work for months. The footage you record could end up saving you hundreds of thousands of dollars, and I've never met a driver who regretted the purchase. It's definitely something to consider if you're worried about driver safety or liability—or if someone close to you is worried about it.

Dash cams can be much more expensive than phone mounts and while I haven't found a perfect camera for ride-share drivers yet, one of the most popular models is the Falcon 360 dual lens dash cam. It has a front-and rear-facing camera to record the interior of the car with adequate night vision in case the lights are off.

This product isn't cheap, ranging from $100–$150 depending on where you buy it, but I like to think of it as an additional insurance policy. Although the odds of ever needing the footage are low, you never know what could go wrong or what you might be held liable for while out on the road.

You can find a full review of different dash cam options on the blog: www.therideshareguy.com/dashcams.

Lots of other products will also aid you in your journey as a rideshare driver. We'll go over those in more detail in chapter 4.

Tracking your miles

A lot of drivers get into this line of work looking to make a few hundred extra dollars a week, but what they don't realize is that they're now a business owner and with the freedom of being their own boss also comes additional reporting requirements.

You don't have to track your miles but if you do, it could mean a huge deduction come tax time. We'll go into more details on rideshare taxes in chapter 8, but for now all you need to know is that for every mile you drive, you'll get to deduct 53.5 cents per mile (which is the IRS Standard Mileage Rate in 2017).

Example: Let's say you earn $100 in a night of driving and you put a total of 100 miles on your car during that time. The IRS will allow you to deduct 53.5 cents per mile or $53.50 (100 miles x $0.535/mile). That means at the end of the year, you'll only have to pay taxes on $46.50 of your income.

There are a few different options when it comes to tracking your mileage. Stride Drive is a great free app for iOS and Android users that tracks your mileage with the tap of a single button, while QuickBooks Self-Employed (QBSE) is a paid app that allows you to track your mileage and get a detailed summary of your profit and loss. It also integrates with TurboTax, so come tax time you should be able to easily import all of your data.

You can sign up for Stride Drive here: www.therideshareguy.com/stridedrive.

You can sign up for QBSE: www.therideshareguy.com/qbse.

Accidents and why you'll want rideshare insurance

Uber and Lyft provide drivers with commercial insurance while you're on a trip or en route to a passenger, but while you're waiting for a request, you may be at risk. This stage is referred to as Period 1 and it occurs when you're online with the Uber app but haven't received a request yet. During this time, Uber and Lyft provide state minimum liability limits but NO collision coverage. If you get into an accident during Period 1, you would be 100 percent responsible for the damage to your car.

Normally, personal insurance would cover you in this situation, but since most personal insurers consider driving for Uber and Lyft commercial activity, they won't provide coverage during Period 1 either.

Here's how the periods break down:[14]

---

14 https://newsroom.uber.com/insurance-for-uberx-with-ridesharing/.

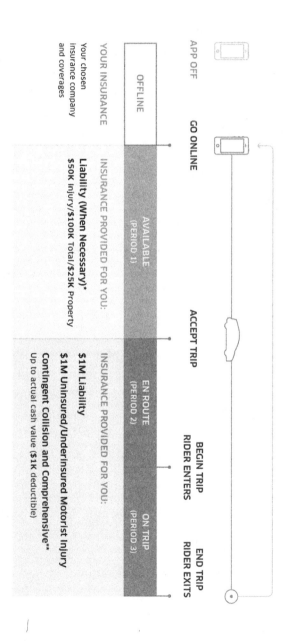

INSURANCE FOR RIDESHARE DRIVERS WITH UBER

APP OFF	GO ONLINE	ACCEPT TRIP	BEGIN TRIP RIDER ENTERS	END TRIP RIDER EXITS

OFFLINE | **AVAILABLE**
(PERIOD 1) | **EN ROUTE**
(PERIOD 2) | **ON TRIP**
(PERIOD 3)

YOUR INSURANCE

Your chosen
insurance company
and coverages

INSURANCE PROVIDED FOR YOU:

Liability (When Necessary)*
$50K Injury/$100K Total/$25K Property

INSURANCE PROVIDED FOR YOU:

$1M Liability
$1M Uninsured/Underinsured Motorist Injury

Contingent Collision and Comprehensive**
Up to actual cash value ($1K deductible)

*   We maintain automobile liability insurance on your behalf if you do not maintain applicable insurance of at least this amount.

** Pays for damage to your vehicle if you maintain auto insurance that includes collision coverage for that vehicle.

Note: Additional coverage will be provided where required by state and local laws. At least this much coverage is provided in all
US states for drivers while operating personal vehicles under the transportation network company model.

In addition to the insurance gap mentioned above, many personal auto insurance companies will drop you from your policy if they find out you're driving for Uber and Lyft. So it's best to look into rideshare insurance if you're considering driving for Uber and Lyft.

Rideshare insurance policies will replace your personal insurance and allow you to work for Uber and Lyft and cover you during Period 1. So if you were to get into an accident during Period 1, your rideshare insurance would be primary. Some companies like State Farm will even cover you during all three periods of rideshare driving so you won't have to rely on Uber's or Lyft's insurance.

In the early days of rideshare, it was tough finding rideshare insurance, but these days most states have multiple providers. Costs and even coverage can vary by company so it's important to get multiple quotes.

You can find a full list of options by state along with recommended agents on our site: www.therideshareguy.com/insurance.

Here's a real-life example of quotes we pulled from four different companies:

Company	State Farm	Mercury	Farmers	Allstate
Six-Month Policy Cost	$981.00	$1,088.00	$844.00	$673.00
Per-Month Policy Cost	$166.00	$273 (First month), $205 monthly	$146.00	$112.95
Period 1 Coverage	Yes	Yes	Yes	Yes

Period 2	Yes	No	No	Deductible Gap Coverage
Period 3	Yes	No	No	Deductible Gap Coverage
Includes Renters Discount	Yes	No (but would be 2 percent)	Yes	No

Assumptions: The car we selected for these quotes was a 2011 Prius (this is the average year, make, and model for drivers in 2017). Each policy offers the same coverage limits, including 100K/300K/100K liability coverage and a $1,000 comprehensive/collision deductible. We assumed an imperfect driving record with two recent speeding tickets. The address provided was Long Beach, California, the DOB was 1987, and marital status was married.

If you ever get into an accident while rideshare driving, you'll provide Uber's or Lyft's insurance information if the accident happened during Period 2 or 3 and your own rideshare insurance if the accident happened during Period 1.

Getting in touch with Uber or Lyft for support

When you're first getting started, you're bound to have some questions about things like the ratings system, how and when you get paid, and more. And unlike a regular job where you can just ask your coworker, with this gig you'll need to figure most things out on your own. Uber provides some training, but for the most part this is a "learn as you go" type of job.

Uber and Lyft both have a reputation for providing poor customer service and it's often one of the major pain points for new drivers. But this book is here to answer all of your questions and for anything left over, you can always send me a personal email at harry@therideshareguy.com and I'll be sure to respond.

There are some issues that only Uber can help with, though. For those, we've got some tips on how to get in contact with Uber. If you're just getting started as a new driver, Uber offers "Greenlight Centers" all across the country. These are in-person support centers where you can get your vehicle inspected, documents approved, and more. Typically, these centers are staffed by Uber employees, so while they may not be as convenient as online or phone support, you will most likely be able to get your questions answered and your issues resolved.

If you have simple questions, Uber provides support in the driver app under the Help tab. You'll need to follow a simple flow depending on the nature of your question and this will allow you to submit an inquiry to Uber. If you're not a driver yet, you can also access help.Uber.com to find answers to your questions.

Lyft also offers in-person support centers called Hubs, but they're not as prevalent. Fortunately, you can also get help through the Lyft driver app and on help.Lyft.com.

Recently, Uber started offering 24/7 phone support that can be accessed from the driver app, so it's definitely getting easier to contact them. For new drivers, Uber also offers live chat support from the app or online in certain cities. Lyft has recently started testing phone support in select cities, too.

If none of the above methods work, both companies are active on social media, which is another way to get help quickly. You can reach Uber or Lyft support on Twitter or send them a message through Facebook.

Ultimately, regardless of which contact method you use, don't forget to follow up. I've never seen a driver get fired for contacting Uber or Lyft too much, so don't worry about that, but be respectful in tone and try to ask questions one at a time with enough detail to get your point across. Not many companies do customer service well, so if you're expecting a lot out of Uber and Lyft, you may be disappointed. Fortunately, there are resources like this book that will provide you almost everything you need.

3
What's it like to give your first ride?

YOU'VE SIGNED UP AND ARE ready for your first ride. It can be intimidating. I was pretty nervous to give my first ride all the way back in 2014, and I remember signing on for the first time and staring at my screen for ten minutes not knowing exactly what to expect.

I was hoping my car would be clean enough and that I would know which buttons to push on my phone in order to accept a ride. I was also hoping I wouldn't get a drunk person.

Is this thing on?

How long do you think it'll take?

I wonder who it will . . .

PING!

A loud noise rang from my phone and a countdown timer appeared on my screen. The ride was a few miles away so I attached my phone to the mount in my car and was off to give the first of many rides.

It can be a bit nerve-wracking when giving your first ride, but you can do a lot to make sure you're well prepared. Once you get the hang of things, you'll wonder why you were ever nervous in the first place.

Christian Perea's first request came from a girl named Jelena and her pick-up spot was twelve minutes away! As he tells it, "I just wanted to get my first ride over with. So I got in my car and sped down to the Bluefoot Bar in San Diego. I picked her and her boyfriend up and drove them to the Padres game.

"Rideshare was still very new at the time, and they were from Germany. I told them flat out that it was my first ride and had absolutely no idea what I was doing. They turned out to be super cool and we ended up having a conversation about how much a driver might be able to earn doing rideshare.

"The ride went well. I didn't run into anything and it turned out my first passenger was interested in driving so we exchanged contact info and I told her that I had a referral code where we could each get some good bonus money from her signing up.

"Over the next few days, I helped her get set up while hoping I would get the bonus money. Maybe I would make a lot of money just from referring drivers instead.

"Fast forward a month later. I'm sitting in the Von's parking lot waiting for a ride with other drivers when a girl walks out to her BMW with a very disappointed look on her face and a bag full of cleaning supplies. She then begins frantically cleaning up puke from the backseat of her silver BMW.

"I said to myself *I bet you she's an Uber driver*. Nobody else would be cleaning puke out of their car at 8PM in a parking lot.

"I had to know if this was Uber-related so I walked over to the girl cleaning the BMW and lo and behold . . . My first passenger was staring back at me. She had just given her first ride."

My number one tip for new drivers

Before you ever hit the road, the best piece of advice that I can give you is to take a ride as a passenger. Not only will you become familiar with the app and how things work from the customer side, but you'll also get to talk to a real-life driver and see how they operate their vehicle.

If you call for a ride and get a 4.9-star-rated driver, it's important to see what they do when you get into the car and, more importantly, what they don't do. If you get a low-rated driver, maybe you notice that they bombard you with questions as soon as you get in, "What's your name?" . . . "What kind of music do you like?" . . . "Want the windows up or down?"

Uber and Lyft actually provide free rides to new passengers, so make sure you sign up using a promo code if you want to save a few bucks.

- Uber free ride[15] for passengers: Use promo code **3e3dg** or go to: therideshareguy.com/passenger/uber.
- Lyft free ride[16] for passengers: Use promo code **Harry757** or go to: therideshareguy.com/passenger/lyft.

You can learn a lot from taking a ride as a passenger, and as you'll soon find out, one of the challenges of this job is that there isn't any real training. Many new drivers feel like they're thrown to the wolves and need to figure things out themselves. For some, that's fine, but for others, you'll have to take the initiative and learn this new craft. You're already on the right track by buying this book!

First ride checklist

Everyone's a little nervous for their first ride, but there are a few things you can do to make sure things go smoothly:

- **Download the Uber or Lyft driver app:** Find the Uber and Lyft driver apps in the Google Play Store for Android, or App Store in iTunes for iOS.
- **Get a phone mount:** Poor navigation is the number one reason for low ratings and if you're staring at your lap the whole time, you can bet that your passenger will notice. So not only will a phone mount

---

15 Uber's offer to new passengers varies by city but usually it's capped at $10–20 per ride.
16 Lyft's offer to new passengers varies by city but usually it's $5–$10 off your first few rides.

make you a safer driver, it will also make it easier to navigate to your destination and ensure passengers don't ding your rating.

- **Start off in familiar territory:** Downtown on New Year's Eve may not be the best time and place to start. Instead, start in a neighborhood that you're familiar with so if you are having problems with following the navigation for example, you will still know your way around. Suburban areas are much easier to pick up and drop off in, and you won't have to deal with throngs of people all looking for their black Prius, so avoid the city if you can at the start.

- **Ease into it:** You don't need to work twelve hours your first time on the road. My first time out I gave just one ride and called it quits. Start slow and get the hang of things before jumping into a full shift.

- **Avoid the party hours:** Friday and Saturday nights tend to be the busiest times to drive, but when you're just getting started, you'll actually want to avoid these times. That way, you can ease into things and you won't have to worry about pukers.

- **Ignore carpool rides and airports:** UberPOOL and Lyft Line add a few degrees of complexity to any ride since now you have multiple passengers to deal with. You can ignore these requests when you're first getting started, and it may be a good idea to stay away from airports for similar reasons.

- **Be yourself:** A lot of drivers worry about what the passenger might think about their driving or their personality, but most passengers only care about getting from point A to B safely and efficiently.

Accepting ride requests

When a ping comes in, you'll have about ten seconds to tap anywhere on the screen and accept the ride request. If, for some reason, you can't or don't want to take the ride, you always have the option of doing nothing and ignoring the request. This will put you back online and available for requests, but if you ignore two to three trips in a row, Uber may put you in "timeout" for ten to fifteen minutes. This means that you won't be sent any new trip requests. If you aren't ready for ride requests, usually it's best to log off the app until you're ready to drive.

Unlike Uber, Lyft has been known to deactivate drivers if your acceptance rate falls below 80 percent, so it's best to accept your Lyft rides when they come in.

You won't know where the passenger is headed until AFTER you arrive at the rider's destination and swipe to accept the trip, but Uber and Lyft do give you some information ahead of time on the accept screen:

- Type of ride: UberX/UberPOOL/UberEATS/etc.
- Surge level (if applicable): 1.2x would mean that you'll get a 20 percent bonus on this ride. The idea behind surge pricing is to adjust the price of rides to match driver supply to rider demand at any given time. During periods of excessive demand when there are many more riders than drivers, or when there aren't enough drivers on the road and customer wait times are long, Uber and Lyft increase their normal fares and drivers get paid more. More info on surge pricing is found in chapter 5.
- ETA (estimated time to arrival): This will tell you how far away the passenger is.

- Passenger rating: Drivers get to rate passengers at the end of every trip and you'll see the passenger's overall rating[17] on the accept screen.

***

17 In some cities like Chicago, city ordinances prevent Uber/Lyft from displaying the passenger rating.

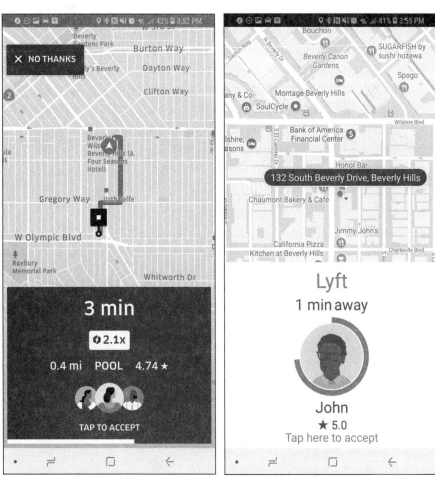

Here's what the request screen will look like on the Uber and Lyft driver apps.

Pro-tip: You can use a third-party app like Mystro (www.therideshareguy.com/mystro) to auto-accept rides for you. We'll learn more about how to leverage apps like Mystro that help drivers earn more in chapter 9.

Once you've accepted a trip, you'll have to drive to your passenger's pick-up location. Uber will notify the passenger when you're one minute away and then again after you've arrived. Once you arrive, Uber will give the rider two minutes to come out before they start charging the per-minute waiting rate. After five minutes of waiting, you have the option of canceling the trip and charging the rider a cancellation fee by selecting that option on your screen. Lyft has a nearly identical acceptance process, although both companies are constantly testing adjustments and new features so you may see something slightly different.

You can contact the rider via Uber's in-app messaging system or call them by selecting the **contact rider** option. Text messages are a lot less obtrusive to customers so I typically avoid calling riders unless they're not coming out or it's an area that is heavily congested and I can't find them.

With Lyft, you can also call your riders but in order to text, you'll need to call them first, hang up quickly (so it doesn't ring on their end) and then use that same phone number to send a text message.

Conducting the ride

Once the passenger is in your vehicle, you will need to swipe the screen to start the trip. Uber and Lyft require passengers to enter their destination ahead of time, so all you should have to do is navigate. While navigation might seem like an easy task, it's actually one of the top reasons drivers get low ratings from passengers. Make sure that you pay close attention to the GPS and navigate your passengers safely to their destination.

Occasionally, I'll verify the general route with the passengers if it's a longer trip, or just to make sure they know which route I'm planning on taking. I've found that a lot of passengers will map the route themselves and "follow along" so if you have a shortcut, you should let them know so they don't wonder where you're going.

One of the most rewarding parts of the job for me are the conversations that you'll have with your passengers. I work at home by myself, so by the end of the day, I'm itching for human contact, and that's typically when I do most of my driving. You'll meet all sorts of different people from every background imaginable while driving for Uber and Lyft.

I always savor the opportunity to talk to someone and learn about who they are, what they do, and where they come from. Driving for Uber provides this opportunity and more. Most rides are fifteen to twenty minutes, so you have just enough time for a deep conversation but it's also hard to get bored.

Some passengers don't want to talk though and that's completely fine. It's up to you as a driver to recognize their body language and tell whether they're in the mood for a chat or not. I typically open with something simple like, "How's your day been?" or "Would you like me to turn on the A/C?" in order to gauge their temperament. If they start yapping away, I know I've got the green light. But if they're just staring at their phone the whole time or putting on their headphones, I let them be.

Ending the ride

At the conclusion of the trip, you'll swipe to end the trip and be asked to rate your passenger. At this point, passengers will also be given the opportunity to rate you and leave a tip. Drivers are required to rate passengers but only about half of all riders will ever leave a rating for the driver.

The average rating for drivers is around 4.8, and in order to stay active on the platform, you'll need a 4.6-star rating. High ratings are important but you shouldn't stress too much about them when you're first getting started. Uber and Lyft cut you some slack during your first fifty rides and won't be as strict with the 4.6 cutoff, but it's always easier to go down than it is to go up.

If you do end up getting deactivated for low ratings, Uber contracts with third-party training companies in select cities, and you can pay around $80–$150 for training and "reactivation." If you're eligible, Uber will send you an email with details a couple weeks after you've been deactivated. There isn't a formal process for getting reactivated, so it's best to avoid getting deactivated for low ratings in the first place if you can at all help it. With Lyft, there's no re-activation process; do your best to maintain a high rating right from the start.

How fares are calculated

Before passengers request a ride, they are quoted an upfront price, and your pay as a driver is based on the mileage and time it takes to get from the pick-up point to the destination. Drivers are not paid for the time and distance it takes to drive to a passenger to pick them up (unless it's an extra-long pickup). Below is an explanation of the different parts of a ride:

- Base fare: This is the amount that Uber charges riders right off the bat. Think of it as a pick-up fee (although most cities do not have a base fare).
- Per mile: From the time you start a trip, until the time you end a trip, you will be compensated for all the miles you drive to the nearest tenth (.10) of a mile. So even if your passenger enters a final destination but wants to continue for another half a mile, as long as you don't end the trip, you will continue to get paid the per-mile rate.
- Per minute: In addition to the per-mile rate, you're also paid a per-minute rate for the entire duration of a trip.
- Per-minute wait time: Passengers don't always come out right when you arrive. In order to incentivize them to hurry up, Uber has recently started charging a per-minute wait time rate after you've arrived at a passenger's location and waited for two minutes.
- Minimum trip earnings: If a passenger goes a short distance and the total earnings (base fare + per minute wait time + per minute rate + per mile rate) are less than the minimum trip earnings, you will automatically be paid the minimum trip earnings. See below for an example of minimum trip earnings in Los Angeles.
- Cancellation fee: If a rider requests a ride and cancels after more than two minutes, you'll receive a cancellation fee. Or if you arrive at a rider's location

and they don't come outside within five minutes, you can cancel the trip and receive a cancellation fee.

- Booking fee: This fee is charged directly to the rider and does not go to the driver.

Let's say a passenger takes a ride from Santa Monica, California, to downtown Los Angeles, and the ride takes thirty-five minutes and comes out to 15.7 miles. In order to calculate your payout, we'll need the current driver rates in Los Angeles, which look like this (as of October 2017):

UberX Driver Payouts - Los Angeles	
Base Fare	$0.00
Per Mile	$0.72
Per Minute	$0.113
Per Minute Wait Time	$0.113
Minimum Trip Earnings	$2.625
Cancellation Fee	$3.75
Booking Fee	$2.10

In order to calculate the driver's pay, we need to do some math:

Base Fare	+	(Miles x Per Mile)	+	(Time x Per Minute)	=	Driver's Pay
$0.00	+	15.7 miles x $0.720/mile	+	35 mins. x $0.113/min	=	Driver's Pay
$0.00	+	$11.30	+	$3.96	=	$15.26

In the past, what the passenger paid was tied to the price the driver would get. As of 2016, Uber has switched to an upfront pricing model where drivers are always paid based off the exact mileage and time (as outlined above), but passengers are quoted an upfront price that can vary from factors like time/traffic and even neighborhood.

The cost to the passenger for this ride would be around $23–31.[18] You can check the rates for your city on partners. uber.com.

Lyft's pay structure is very similar and in most cities, the rates are identical to Uber. When I told you earlier that these companies like to copy each other, I wasn't kidding.

App and phone troubleshooting

When you are going out to drive, I find it best to restart your phone to give it a fresh slate to work from. Running all the apps you need at the same time puts a strain on the phone, so you want to clear out all the apps you won't need.

I also restart my phone after I take a break so any social media, email, games, etc. I might be using during my break are not active when I go back driving again. For me, this helps keep the phone running smoothly. That means you won't miss any trips and your navigation app will work when you need it to.

If you're still running into issues, it may be that you are on an older phone and typically, newer phones work best for rideshare drivers since you're running multiple apps and constantly using your phone.

---

18   https://www.uber.com/cities/los-angeles.

4

How can you become a five-star driver?

WHEN I FIRST STARTED DRIVING for Uber, I luckily got off to a pretty hot start when it came to my driver rating. I maintained my five-star rating for the first two weeks but one morning, after a full night of driving, I checked my app and saw that I had dropped all the way down to a 4.9 rating!

I was devastated since I felt like I had provided great service and even worse, there wasn't a way to tell what I had done wrong! Over time, I've come to accept that low ratings are a part of the game, but it can still be frustrating for a lot of new drivers since like many of you, I take pride in my level of service.

You might frequent four-star rated restaurant on Yelp and TripAdvisor, but a four-star rated Uber driver is going to be fired! So while you can't fret about every low rating you get, a high rating is of utmost importance since it will ensure that you don't lose your job.

How do you maintain that five-star rating and what are the secrets?

How the ratings system actually works

The first thing you'll need to understand is how drivers are rated and why. At the end of every trip, passengers are asked to rate drivers on a scale from 1 to 5. Uber will take the average of your last five hundred rated trips and come up with an overall driver rating.

It's important to maintain at least a 4.6 when you're just getting started, but you shouldn't stress too much about your rating. With time, you'll get better and slowly improve your ratings. And if you're nervous or unsure of anything, don't be afraid to let your passenger know that you're new and they should cut you some slack.

After you've done a couple hundred trips, individual ratings won't affect your score nearly as much since you'll have a much larger sample size to go off of. Still, it can be frustrating to get low ratings since you don't always know why it's happening.

Lyft takes an average of your last hundred trips, so if you have a bad rating or two, it will have a bigger impact on your overall rating, but they'll also drop off your record a lot quicker.

Unfortunately, Uber and Lyft don't share who left what rating for privacy reasons so at times, it can be hard to know what you're doing wrong. You're also not allowed to challenge specific ratings so even though I still get frustrated by low ratings, over time I've come to accept it. The ratings system has its flaws but at the end of the day, it does ensure that drivers and riders are held accountable for their actions.

What matters most for high ratings

Getting five stars is a lot simpler than you might think. Uber has studied passenger ratings and told drivers that the number one reason for a low rating from a passenger has to do with safe driving and navigation. But what does that mean?

Safe driving might seem like a no-brainer, but the way you drive on your own might be a lot different than how you should be driving with passengers in the car. My best advice is to drive like your toddler is in the backseat. Would you run that yellow light if you had a baby on board? Probably not. Would you tail other cars and slam on the brakes if you had a baby in the backseat? Probably not.

It might seem like common sense, but this job is really about putting yourself in other people's shoes and understanding that their safety and comfort is paramount, not yours. Following directions from a navigation app isn't too tough of a job on its own, but remember that safe driving and navigation always come first! It might be fun to chat up your passenger, but conversation should never get in the way of your driving. I like to practice using navigation when I'm not driving for Uber or Lyft since that allows me to focus on that aspect of driving. After a few weeks of this, you should be able to approximate how far 450 feet is or 0.1 miles so you know when to exit or take that left turn without even having to look at your app.

Calvin Hill is an Uber driver out of Atlanta, Georgia, who has built a massive YouTube following because of his in-depth videos and extensive rideshare knowledge. He publishes Uber videos under the brand name, "The Simple Driver." His videos highlight having great business acumen, and that strong navigation skills is one of the most important ways to make more money and get higher ratings. Knowing where to go and how to get there efficiently is key and can make the difference between a high and low rating. The Simple Driver recommends using Waze, but you can also use Google Maps as well to make sure that your navigation is on point.

Passengers regularly ask drivers how long it takes to get to a destination and the Simple Driver recommends you give them the exact time instead of a guess-timate. How can you be sure? With Google Maps, Waze, or your favorite map app, you can give them the exact time when they will arrive at their destination and confirm their preferred route. This will help you look like a five-star driver since Google Maps and Waze have already done the hard work for you in determining if accidents or construction are blocking the road, and their estimations of arrival time are very accurate.

Know your area's top landmarks and the basics

It's easy to rely on technology but you don't want to blindly follow and do whatever the navigation tells you to. There's a famous scene in one of my favorite TV comedies, *The Office*, where the boss, Michael, is following his GPS and it tells him to veer left. Michael blindly takes its advice and ends up in the bottom of the lake.

This is an extreme example, but the same concept applies to driving for Uber. Sometimes, you may be in rural areas where your GPS signal gets lost, or you may be downtown among all the skyscrapers and your GPS thinks you are four blocks over.

In either scenario, it's important to understand the basics of directional navigation and your area's top landmarks. You should know which way North, East, South, and West are so that if your GPS or navigation is on the fritz, you can at least start heading in the right direction and once you get service again, your app will automatically correct itself.

You'll also find that a majority of drop-offs are going to be in the same general areas, and the same bars or restaurants tend to keep popping up on the app. I always tell new drivers that they should spend some time on Wikipedia for their city and memorize the top three to five landmarks, tourist sites, restaurants, and bars.

Once you've done a couple weeks of driving, you'll have a good beat on the top destinations and can memorize those locations, too. That way, if anything ever goes wrong GPS-wise, the app is malfunctioning, or you don't have service, you can just ask the passenger where they're going and there's a decent chance you'll know which part of town it is.

Tips and how to get them

Uber and Lyft both allow passengers to leave a tip in the app at the completion of their ride. These tips will go 100 percent to the driver and no commission is taken from them. Unlike taxis or other service industries, you won't get tipped on most of your rides but that doesn't mean it can't add a nice bonus to your income.

Some drivers think that providing extras like gum or water will help boost their ratings or their tips but we know that safe driving and navigation trump a piece of candy any day of the week. You can be a five-star rated driver without ever handing out a single amenity.

That being said, it can't hurt to go the extra mile when you're just getting started. Some drivers struggle with learning the app and following navigation so while you get your bearings, it may make sense to provide an enhanced experience in other areas for your passenger. That way, if you make any mistakes, your rider may be a little kinder when leaving a rating.

Usually, there's a strong correlation between high ratings and high tips. I prefer providing amenities like iPhone and Android charging cables since these are one-time investments that pay ongoing dividends.

What it all boils down to is standing out from the competition—what can you do as a driver that other drivers aren't doing? Charging cables and AUX cords (so passengers can play music from their own phone) are no-brainer investments since they're cheap and reusable, but I also like to focus on providing service that is better than other drivers.

When I'm sitting at a stoplight, I'll look at the passenger's final destination and see if it's on the right side or left side of the street and ask them where they'd like to be dropped off. These are the things I care about as a passenger and, again, why it's so important to take a ride as a passenger from time to time.

I've also found that meaningful conversation can lead to great tips. As I mentioned earlier, I love learning about new people and I try to educate myself on various current events, sports, technology, and more so that I can have intelligent conversations with my passengers. But I don't partake in these conversations to try and get more tips. Sure, it's a nice by-product, but I'm genuinely curious about my passengers' lives and I'm always eager to listen and learn from them.

The only caveat here is that I'd try and avoid politics and religion since opinions can vary there!

Here are some more products and services that can help you as a driver

The nice thing about Uber is that you don't have to buy anything extra to become a driver, but there are a few products that will greatly improve your experience, passengers' experience, and your rating, and will hopefully get you some tips in the process.

Must-haves:

- Phone mount: Nobody wants a driver who's staring at their lap every few seconds. Get a solid $10–$30 phone mount and then you'll be able to safely operate your device and follow navigation hands-free.
- Charging cables: I keep my cables dangling neatly into the backseat and passengers are always appreciative of them.
- Dash camera: A good two-way dash cam will cost you $100–$150, but I like to think of it as a cheap insurance policy. You never know what could go wrong and dash cam footage could be used to prove your side of the story in any type of accident or incident.
- Google Maps or Waze: Uber has their own in app navigation system, but I recommend using a

third-party app like Google Maps or Waze since it's a lot more accurate and it's what passengers often use themselves. If you have the apps installed, you can select either option in the settings of the Uber driver app and every time you hit **Navigate**, the Uber driver app will open up your preferred navigation app. Lyft's driver app now integrates directly with Google Maps so you can navigate as normal from within the app and it will use Google Maps' data.

Probably should-haves:

- Car wash membership: Look for a local car wash that has a cheap monthly plan for unlimited car washes in your area. A lot of car washes cater to rideshare drivers. If you can find one with vacuums, even better.
- Microfiber cloth: A cheap cloth to wipe down the dust on your car will keep it looking new in between washes.
- Floor mats: Driving hundreds of strangers around every week will track a lot of dirt and foreign objects into your car. I keep high-quality rubber floor mats in my car so that I can just shake them out at the end of every day.

Optional:

- Water, gum, mints, and candy: These extras definitely won't hurt your rating, but some passengers may leave wrappers behind and/or cause a mess.
- Handheld vacuum: This is a good way to keep your car clean in between car washes and get you moving when you have downtime between rides.

- AUX cord: Some drivers don't want drunk passengers blasting music, but for me it's all part of the experience (and can help with tips and ratings).

JT Genter is a full-time travel writer and has experience as both an Uber driver and Uber passenger. A lot of his best advice for drivers has to do with staying in constant communication with your passenger.

JT says that as a driver, it's important to accommodate your passenger's pick-up zones and, as long as it's legal, do your best to get to their location. He also mentions texting or calling your passenger. Particularly if your rider is running late, you may want to call and make sure they're still coming and they know where your car is instead of waiting for them to find you. Doing something simple like this lets the passenger know you're there and helps them find you easier—getting you on the trip faster.

5

How do I maximize my profits?

So now you've signed up, learned the ropes, given a few rides, and gotten some good feedback from passengers. It's time to start making some real money.

One of the things I like most about driving for Uber is that there's a strong correlation between how hard you work and how much money you're making. If you want to work sixty to eighty hours a week, you're free to do that and your pay will reflect the increased hours. But it's not all about working harder, it's also about working smarter.

Unlike other retail or service jobs, Uber has no minimum wage and no set pay. If you were to hire five new workers at Starbucks as baristas, they'd all make the exact same amount per hour, and it'd probably be a while before they were eligible for a raise, if at all. But if you take five Uber drivers and let them loose, you're going to see a ton of variability.[19] Some might make $20–$30 an hour and others may barely make minimum wage. So why the discrepancy? Simply put, when and where you drive matters and savvy drivers will earn more money than those wandering around aimlessly waiting for a ping.

When you should drive

When you're just getting started, the income you make isn't as important as getting used to your driving schedule and learning the basics of rideshare driving. You'll want to find the times and places to drive that work well with your schedule but also that line up with the busiest times of demand.

If you love driving weekday afternoons, you can do that, but that also correlates with times of lowest demand, so you probably won't make nearly as much as if you were to drive other times.

Taking advantage of Uber's Surge Pricing and Lyft's Prime Time

To maximize your per-hour income, you'll want to take advantage of surge pricing. Surge pricing refers to the system Uber has put in place to ensure there's always enough supply (drivers) to meet demand (riders). During busy times, Uber dynamically raises the price that a rider is asked to pay in order to entice more drivers onto the road.

In the past, riders would have to physically accept a

---

19   http://therideshareguy.com/which-cities-do-uber-drivers-make-the-most-money-in/.

higher surge price, but now Uber presents an upfront price to the rider that is inclusive of all surge and other taxes and fees. On the driver's side, we still see surge levels on the accept screen when the ride request comes in.

If we revisit our example from chapter 3, an Uber driver gave a ride that lasted 15.7 miles and thirty-five minutes and the driver was paid $15.26. Now let's say a surge multiplier of 2.0x was applied to that ride. That means that the driver will now get double his or her pay.

So $15.24 ride x 2.0 Surge = **$30.52**

The nice thing about surge is that drivers do the exact same amount of work yet are paid double, triple, or sometimes even more—when it's really busy! Lyft uses a similar system to balance supply and demand but it's referred to as Prime Time. It works just like surge but instead of a multiplier, Lyft uses a percentage-based system where 100 percent Prime Time means you'll get 100 percent extra.

So if you get a $15 ride and there is 100 percent PT, that means you'll earn $30. And if you want to convert PT to surge, here is how it will look:

100% Prime Time = 2.0x Surge
200% Prime Time = 3.0x Surge
400% Prime Time = 5.0x Surge

So how do you find surge and Prime Time?

Surge is indicated on the driver app by hexagons that are varying shades of red. Pink usually indicates a 1–2.0x surge while the darker the red, the higher the surge amount will be.

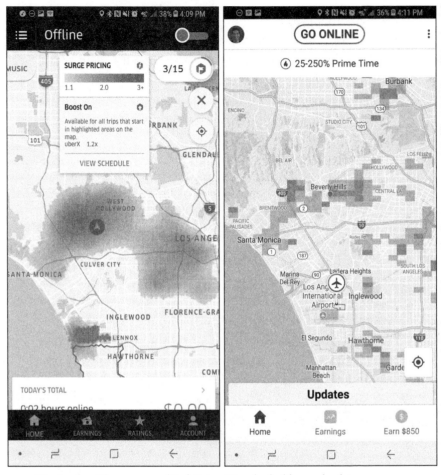

Here's what Uber surge and Lyft Prime Time looks like on the driver apps.

As a new driver, it can be tempting to chase the surge and drive toward it but that's actually a huge mistake! Surge is dynamic so if an area is surging, and hundreds of drivers flock toward the dark red areas, that increases the supply of drivers and the surge will naturally drop.

That doesn't mean you should avoid surge completely. Savvy drivers know that the best way to take advantage of surge is to understand when and where it's going to surge so you can position yourself accordingly. Here are some times where surge pricing is common:

- Friday/Saturday nights: Demand from riders always peaks on the weekends and this is typically when you'll see the highest levels of surge. If you can make it until bar closing time (2 a.m. in most jurisdictions), you may be rewarded with lots of surge.
- Big events: Concerts, festivals, and sports are great opportunities for surge since thousands of people are trying to request rides all at the same time.
- Holidays: New Year's Eve and Halloween have typically been the busiest days of the year to drive.

In order to really maximize your earnings, you'll need to take advantage of surge. It's important to remember that it's made up of two components: driver supply and rider demand. A lot of the best times meet one or both of those criteria.

You can keep an eye on Uber's surge pricing without even going online on the Uber driver app. Open up your app and zoom in to check the surge levels around town. Some drivers will even take this a step further and use two phones while driving: one phone to drive for Uber or Lyft, and the other phone to zoom out to your entire market to watch the surge areas.

One of the best pieces of advice I can give you in your pursuit of earning more money is to "Follow the Alcohol." Most people rely on rideshare services when they want to consume alcohol, so Friday and Saturday nights are typically the best times to drive. There are some downsides since you'll have to drive around a bunch of drunks, but the income usually makes up for it!

Here are some other winning strategies for Uber and Lyft drivers:

Commuting Hours

The second busiest time to drive is during weekday commuting hours. More and more people are ditching their cars in favor of rideshare, but they still need to get to work every day. So we typically see demand spike during the morning rush hour (8–10 a.m.) and then again in the afternoon (4–6 p.m.).

You can take advantage of the increased rides, but you'll also have to deal with traffic since lots of other cars are on the road. Since the per-mile payout is multiples higher than the per-minute payout, you always want to be on the move. You can't do a whole lot about this during rush hour but it's important to keep in mind.

Early A.M. Airport Rides

Not many drivers are willing to get up at 3 or 4 a.m., but if you are a morning person, you could be rewarded with long rides and no traffic. Airport rides have always been profitable for drivers since many airports are located twenty to thirty minutes outside of city centers and that's the sweet spot when it comes to time and distance.

If you live in the suburbs, you may even find that you can catch rides to the airport before you even leave your house. Before I head out, I like to turn my app on while I'm still at home and doing a few things around the house until I get my first call.

Walk of Shame Rides

A lot of drivers and riders stay out late on Friday and Saturday nights, which creates the perfect storm in the morning. Most drivers are sleeping from the night before, yet a number of passengers who had a little too much fun the night prior still need a ride home.

You can typically find these rides around 8 to 10 a.m., and there's often intermittent surge to boot. Whenever I don't feel like driving the party hours, I make sure that I'm available the next morning since there's often no traffic and the riders are calm and quiet (a.k.a. hungover).

Special Events

Big cities have dozens of events and activities going on every day, but regardless of the size of your city, there's likely a whole host of events waiting for you. I like to use apps like EventBrite or StubHub in order to see what's going on in my city, but usually sporting events, concerts, and festivals can be profitable for drivers since there tends to be lots of surge pricing. Here are some examples:

- Pro sporting events: Most mid to major cities have at least one professional team and often times many more.
- College football: This is a spectacle in itself and even many small towns have college football teams that will attract thousands of riders.
- Concerts: During the off-season, there's a good chance that your local sports venues host dozens of concerts. But don't forget about the smaller venues too, since shows even with a few hundred people could generate significant demand.
- Music festivals: We've seen a huge increase in the number of music festivals every year and although you may have heard of big ones like Coachella and Lollapalooza, more are popping up all the time.

Holidays

Whether it's New Year's Eve, July 4, or Halloween, most holidays revolve around drinking, and that means lots of rides for Uber and Lyft drivers. I've always tried to focus my driving efforts on the most profitable times to drive and big holidays have been essential to that plan.

The major downside to this strategy is that you won't get to spend time with your family or friends, but you can also take a hybrid approach like I've done in the past.

Although the money from rideshare driving is nice, the best part of being a rideshare driver for me has always been the flexibility. But after a few months of driving, I noticed that some of the most profitable holidays to drive were cutting into my social life. So, one year on July 4, I went for the best of both worlds: I wanted to drive and make as much as I could, but I also wanted to spend time with family and friends.

My strategy was to drive the night before July 4, early on the fourth, and then on July 5 in the morning. That first evening ended up being a very good night—not only was there a surge (fewer drivers than there were passengers), but there was also an Uber guarantee of $35/hour.

On the big holiday, I started giving rides early near the beach as parking is usually in short supply and I ended up making $40 an hour over a period of four hours from 9 a.m. to 1 p.m. The best part of all is that I still had plenty of time to go hang out and celebrate the Fourth of July with friends and family. Being a rideshare driver is all about balance for me. I could have worked the entire holiday weekend and made more money, but I would have missed out on a lot of quality time with my friends and family. Luckily, I didn't have to choose one or the other.

You can listen to my podcast episode about this weekend to learn more about the strategies I used at therideshareguy.com/episode4

Experiment with new times and places

A lot of drivers are creatures of habit so it's easy to get into a routine and stick with it. But driving for Uber and Lyft is a dynamic enterprise since the only constant in this industry is change. You'll need to adjust your driving style accordingly.

One of the best discoveries I ever made during an experiment was the early morning airport runs. Living in LA, I abhor traffic, and one day I decided to get up at 4 a.m. and turn on my app to see how busy it was. It turns out that one of the only reasons for riders to request a ride at that time is so they can head to the airport. There aren't a lot of requests at this time but there also aren't a lot of drivers, so I always find myself with nice long rides and no traffic.

Bonuses, incentives, and more!

We covered sign-up bonuses in chapter 1, but over the past few years, weekly bonuses and incentives have started to make up a bigger portion of driver pay. Unfortunately, these bonuses aren't as prevalent in the smaller markets. If you live in a busy market like Los Angeles, New York, San Francisco, or Chicago, weekly bonuses will be important to your driving strategy.

Uber has tested several different weekly bonus structures in the past (and will likely continue to do so), but the basics of these programs are what we'll focus on in this book. Lyft uses similar incentive programs, but in order to confuse you, they have different names for them.

How does Uber Quest Work?

Uber Quest is a driver incentive program that pays a reward when a driver completes a certain number of trips within a certain time period. In the example below, a $60 reward is offered for completing fifteen trips and meeting certain other requirements.

While Uber doesn't release information on exactly how they match drivers with Quest offers, it seems the offers are based on a blend of market demand and previous driver behavior. We also know that Quest bonuses can vary from driver to driver even within the same market. I wouldn't lose too much sleep over the offers you get, though, as it's not really in your control.

When it comes to driving for Uber, it's always a good idea to look at the fine print for offers like this. The requirements may vary slightly depending on your market, but here are the requirements for a typical Quest Promo.

Time period: Each Quest incentive will have a specific time period in which the required trips must be completed. Normally, each week there will be an incentive period for weekdays that goes from 4 a.m. Monday to 4 a.m. Friday. Come the weekend, there's a second incentive period from 4 a.m.

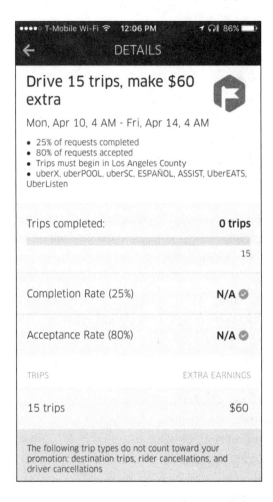

Friday to 4 a.m. Monday. I usually receive an email from Uber the night before the incentive period starts, urging me to check my app for the latest offers.

Completion rate: A 25 percent completion rate is required. This means that I must complete at least 25 percent of the trip requests I accept. This requirement should be easy for most drivers to meet.

Acceptance rate: An 80 percent acceptance rate is also required. So out of all of the Uber requests sent to my phone while I'm online, I must accept 80 percent in order to qualify. This requirement can be a little trickier to meet. I might not want to accept a request if the pickup is far away, the passenger rating is low, or the surge or boost multiplier is not as high as I'd like. But if I want to cash in on the Quest bonus, I better be sure to keep my acceptance rating above the required threshold.

Starting point: For my Quest offers, all trips must begin within the county lines. Check your app for required starting points in your market.

Trip types: Many types of trips qualify for Quest, including UberX, UberPOOL, and even UberEATS (we'll learn more about UberEATS in chapter 9). This is great for drivers because it gives us options to earn incentives while completing a variety of types of trips. I can complete rides during rush hour and food deliveries during meal times, with each trip counting toward my total. And while UberPOOL tends to be a pain point with drivers, the good news is that each Pool pickup counts to your Quest total. So, an UberPOOL ride with three pickups and drop-offs would count as three trips when it comes to reaching your goal.

Excluded from Quest: Rider cancellations and driver cancellations do NOT count toward Quest promotions. You can still earn cancellation fees, but they will not increase your trip total in terms of Quest.

Earnings Boost
The gist of this program is that it offers drivers guaranteed surge pricing on fares that originate from a certain area at

a certain time while charging the passenger regular pric-
es. These promotions tend to be offered in bigger markets
where Lyft is most competitive, but we've also seen them
rolling out in other places too.

There's no need to opt-in for Uber Earnings Boost, but
in order to be eligible you must receive the offer via an email
from Uber. If, for some reason, you didn't get the email or
just ignored it, you'll also see a display for Uber Earnings
Boost within the driver partner app while on the road.

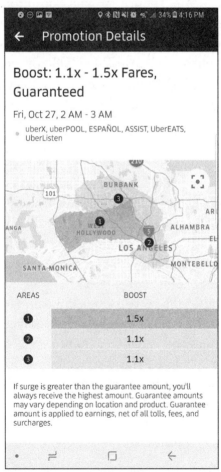

Here's what a typical Earnings Boost Promotion will look like on the Uber Driver App.

The time Uber Earnings Boost will be available will be listed in the email or the app. The email will display all the Uber Earnings Boost times for the week, while the in-app notification will display what Uber Boost is for the current day.

Typically, earning boosts happen during the times when they're trying to incentivize drivers to get out on the road: rush hour/commuting hours and weekend night party hours. And the boost amounts during the times of higher demand are also higher. You'll notice earnings boosts follow the same logic as surge pricing.

The Boost Area should also display on your app in a red outline when the boost is available (it won't show up during non-boost times or if you didn't receive the offer). Any rides originating from within the red boundaries of the app will automatically have a surge multiplier attached to them.

If there is natural surge within the area of the Boost while it's in effect, you will get paid whichever one is higher.

Lyft also offers weekly incentives. Instead of a per-trip bonus like Uber's Quest, they are currently offering weekly guarantees where drivers are guaranteed certain earnings if they maintain a 90 percent acceptance rate and complete a specified number of trips.

For example, the current offer in Los Angeles for Lyft's weekly guarantee is $375 in guaranteed earnings if you complete thirty rides and maintain a 90 percent acceptance rate. This number is before Lyft's commission, so it's the total of your gross fares and tips. Each week, Lyft sends out new offers to drivers via email and in the app to those in certain cities.

Lyft Power Driver Bonus

Lyft's flagship bonus program is called the Power Driver Bonus and if you meet all the requirements you can receive additional earnings. Below are the typical requirements:

- Region: Power Driver Bonus must be available in your region.
- Vehicle: Cars must be a 2011 model or newer to be eligible for Power Driver Bonus. More than half of the rides in a week must be with an eligible vehicle.
- Rides: You must meet the ride requirements in your Driver Dashboard. These requirements may include giving a certain number of peak rides.
- Acceptance rate: You must have a 90 percent acceptance rate for the week.

Lyft uses a tiered ride structure for the Power Driver Bonus and basically, the more rides you do, the more money you'll get.

The only problem with bonus offers like these is that it makes it difficult to drive more than one platform. There's some debate among drivers as to whether you can make more by just doing bonuses on one app or by driving for multiple apps, but it really depends on the offers you're receiving.

I'd suggest tracking your income for a couple weeks on bonuses and then doing the same while driving for Uber and Lyft at the same time. The bonuses are nice but the problem with this strategy is that if you become too reliant on them, Uber and Lyft can always lower the amounts or pull them completely in your market.

Driving for both Uber and Lyft

A lot of drivers get started with either Uber or Lyft but it isn't long before they add a second service. In our most recent survey of over 1,100 drivers,[20] we found that over 67 percent of drivers have signed up for more than one company, and that percentage should go up in the future as it gets easier to work for multiple companies at once.

If you're just getting started, you don't need to add another company to your repertoire yet. Take your time and learn the ropes with just one first. Once you've done fifty rides or so and gotten the hang of things, then it's time to start thinking about adding another service.

There are a lot of reasons why you'll want to work for multiple services, but one of the most important reasons is diversification. If you've ever talked to a financial advisor, you probably know that it isn't a good idea to put all of your money into a single stock since if it goes belly up, you'll lose all your money. It's better to diversify and spread out the risk, and the same is true with rideshare.

If you make 100 percent of your income from Uber, you're really at their mercy when it comes to nearly everything. If they lower rates or change policies, you'll have to go with the flow. If they temporarily deactivate you due to an expired document or their app goes down, you won't have a way to make money. So even if you get most of your rides with Uber, it still makes sense to have Lyft or another service as a backup. Since you never know what could happen, it's better to be over-prepared than underprepared.

---

20   therideshareguy.com/rsg-2017-survey-results-driver-earnings -satisfaction-and-demographics/.

As an independent contractor, you can work for multiple services, but the logistics of doing it will take some practice. You'll have to apply to drive with each company separately but once you're approved, you have the ability to log on to both apps and be available for ride requests at the same time.

The reason why you'll want to do this is to increase your chances of getting a ride—especially during the slower times. If it's busy out, it might seem like it's easier to just stick with one app. But as we learned in chapter 5, you can increase your earnings by filtering out certain passenger requests. Although it's more of an advanced strategy, it almost always makes more sense to drive both Uber and Lyft at the same time.

One thing you'll need to decide on is what you'll do with your trade dress. Trade dress are the stickers that Uber and Lyft send you to put on the lower corner of the passenger side of your windshield. I recommend putting Uber and Lyft trade dress vertically stacked on top of each other as seen below. Passengers are generally aware that many drivers do both Uber and Lyft, so it shouldn't cause any problems. Uber and Lyft also don't have a problem with you showing both companies' trade dress on your window, since you're an independent contractor.

Some drivers like to use two phones when they drive for both companies and they'll run Uber on one phone and Lyft on the other, but I don't find that to be necessary—especially now that apps like Mystro (which we'll learn about in chapter 9), will automate the process of driving for both Uber and Lyft.

Ignoring rides to boost your bottom line

The topics discussed in this next section can sometimes be controversial, but I'll let you decide what's okay and what isn't. The thing you need to keep in mind is that nobody cares about your earnings more than you do. Uber and Lyft want drivers to make money and stay happy, but their profits are always going to come first.

Rideshare is a two-sided marketplace, but the system isn't perfect and there are times where drivers may be asked to go out of their way for no financial reward. Uber has done more than Lyft to fix this in the past couple years but situations and rides still come up that may cost you money as a driver if you accept them.

The best advice I can give you when it comes to being a more cutthroat rideshare driver is that you don't have to take every ride. Uber and Lyft send drivers ride requests, but legally they can not deactivate you for ignoring requests. That being said, if you ignore two or three rides in a row, you may be put in a ten- to fifteen-minute time-out.

Ignoring UberPOOL Rides (and Lyft Line)
Over the past few years, UberPOOL has become a popular option among riders on the Uber platform. UberPOOL is a

service that is similar to UberX but it matches groups of one or two passengers headed in similar directions, saving the passenger up to 40 percent of the cost of the ride.

Drivers have never been big fans of the service since you get paid about the same for double the work. Pickups and drop-offs are the most challenging part of the gig and on UberPOOL, you have to do it twice. When we surveyed drivers in Los Angeles, 75 percent of them reported that they were dissatisfied with their POOL experience. So what can you do about it?

Many drivers (including yours truly) ignore POOL requests completely unless I'm on a Quest bonus (since Pool rides count toward your Quest bonus). Alternatively, if you decide to take POOL rides, you can always stop new requests after you get your first passenger request in order to prevent Uber from adding more POOL riders. You can stop new requests by heading to the Help menu after you've accepted a ride request and going offline.

On YouTube, Randy Shear is known by his alter ego, UberMan, and he was one of the pioneers of rideshare video blogging. UberMan has years of driving experience under his belt and a loyal following of over forty thousand drivers on his channel. One of his best pieces of advice has to do with UberPOOL.

UberMan dislikes UberPOOL rides so much that he recommends that drivers ignore UberPOOL rides completely. You can do so by merely not tapping accept on the request screen when a ride comes through. This strategy has pros and cons, but one big problem with UberPOOL is that it can distract you as a driver by introducing a new element (a new person to pick up while you're driving) into what can already be a busy environment. Imagine it's raining, you're in traffic talking to a passenger and navigating—and then ping! A new UberPOOL request that has you make an exit you weren't anticipating making.

While Uber has worked hard to fix the issues with UberPOOL, UberMan and many others find it distracting and not worth the effort for the small amount of extra pay they receive as a driver.

You can listen to our interview with UberMan at therideshareguy.com/episode43.

This strategy of ignoring rides won't work as well on Lyft because they have more stringent policies on acceptance rate, but in my book, Lyft Line is just as bad as UberPOOL.

When it's slow, you can't be too picky—you'll need to take almost any ride that comes in. When it's busy, you can have a lot of control over the rides you'll take. As discussed in chapter 3, Uber doesn't tell you where the passenger is headed but you do know how far away they are—this is referred to as the passenger's ETA.

Uber will approximate how long it will take for you to reach your rider, and since this time/mileage is unpaid (unless it's an extra-long pickup), you want this number to be as low as possible. One of the things I've found while driving is that even when it's busy, you can still get six to ten minute ETA requests. In this situation, I'll often ignore any ride that's six or more minutes away in the hopes of getting a request that's five minute ETA or less. Depending on how busy your market is, you may not be able to use this strategy as often, but you can start to see how it would benefit you.

Long rides

In some markets, Uber now offers a feature that notifies drivers of long rides (more than an hour), but if you arrive at a rider's location, start the trip, and see that the rider's destination is an hour away, what would you do? The first thing to understand is that you never have to do a ride[21] and you can always end the trip at any point. Let's say you get a one-hour ride request that's going to put you in a location that's in the middle of nowhere and you'll have to drive back empty to the city. A lot of drivers will take this ride but you always have the option of telling the rider, in the nicest way possible, why you can't do that ride.

This obviously isn't the best experience for all parties involved, and you will likely receive a low rating from the passenger, but if you're a highly rated driver, the low rating shouldn't affect you much and you might easily save yourself a lot of time and money. Another time you may want to consider this strategy is if you're on a Quest bonus and the ride will take you outside of the bonus zone.

---

21 Unless the law deems it necessary, as in the case of a service animal.

6

How should I deal with difficult passengers and challenging situations?

So now you're driving for Uber and Lyft, following the advice in this book, and doing everything you can to make your and your passengers' experience positive (and lucrative for you). But some things are always going to be out of your control on the road and challenging situations are bound to arise no matter what you do.

One day, while rideshare driving, I was stopped at a red light when all three of my passengers stripped down to their underwear and got out of the car, ran around the outside and switched seats. It was an old-fashioned Chinese Fire Drill and it turns out that they had lost a bet and this was their punishment.

Alcohol can make people do strange things, and you're bound to encounter some interesting situations while driving for Uber and Lyft. Drunken shenanigans like these are easy to laugh off and, in fact, most rides go off without a hitch. But if you drive long enough, you're probably going to encounter a few that cross the line and make you a little uncomfortable or may even become too unruly.

A lot of the crazy stories you may have heard or seen in the news typically involve alcohol and late-night driving, so some drivers try to avoid them completely by only driving during the day. Even then, it's best to be prepared.

Be the captain of your own ship

Even though I affectionately refer to Friday and Saturday nights as the party hours, it's not as crazy as you might think. Yes, a lot of passengers have been drinking but for the most part, they're respectful and will follow your rules if you establish that you are the one who's in charge.

Passengers prefer a driver who is confident and competent in what they are doing. They are paying for the convenience of being shuttled from A to B and to make the hassle of transport disappear.

The thing is, there is really no way to train drivers for every type of situation that may come up on the road (and it's actually illegal for Uber to train their independent contractors). So drivers often find themselves making decisions on the fly and there isn't a chance to shoot off a quick email to the company you are driving for asking for help.

Being able to make a confident decision in real time is very important. A lot of this develops with experience on the road, and the right decision is based on what the laws are in your city and what will protect your business. For example, many cities require permits in order to drop off and pick up passengers at airports. If you were to drop off a passenger without a permit and get caught by the airport police, you will receive a large fine and it will be your fault and responsibility to pay that ticket.

At the end of the day, you are the one in charge of your car. This means that you can operate how you wish within the confines of ratings, cancellations, and acceptance rates. Being a competent captain, though, also requires knowing when to be assertive and to make decisions and take risks based on your view of the situation.

I hear a lot of stories about picking up rowdy passengers who are disrespectful toward cars and drivers even though the driver knows in advance that the ride is going to be bad. Many describe the incident by saying, "I knew when I called them that they were going to be trouble."

> **Pro-tip**: If you get a bad attitude over the phone, then you will get a bad attitude when they are in your car. Cancel the ride!

Passengers are not entitled to your property once they call you for a ride. They have no right to damage it or force you to do anything you are uncomfortable with. Simply put, you have a right to refuse to drive them. That "funny feeling" is your past experience telling you not do it!

Example: Some passengers have open containers when they first approach the car. Most will get rid of them if you simply ask them to. Often, it's not even the guy who ordered the ride, but one of his friends. Other times they will offer a "tip" to break the law (don't accept it).

So what should you do?

Many of these situations have turned out to be my best rides and customers (obviously the ones who got rid of the open containers). Others not so much. While there's no right answer, being rude about it probably isn't going to help.

Here are some suggestions if you get a passenger who's trying to enter your car with an open alcohol container:

- If you're funny, crack a joke and say something like, "You can only bring that in my car if you've got one for me." And then casually ask them if they mind throwing out the alcohol. That is one way of defusing the situation.
- If you're not that funny, just let them know you're more than happy to wait until they finish their drink. That way, you avoid telling them outright, "you can't do that," and put the onus on them. Most passengers aren't going to want to wait around so they'll throw the drink out.
- If you don't want to say anything, exit the vehicle and open the door for your passengers before they get in. Most passengers won't try to sneak a beer into the car if you're standing right there in front of them.

Remember that you are the captain of your own ship and this means you're personally responsible for every aspect of driving. That involves knowing the local laws, taking matters into your own hands, and being respectful yet assertive. Everything else will fall in line.

Dash cams can help

If you're worried about transporting strangers around, one of the best things you can do for yourself is get a dash cam. You'll want to make sure you follow all the local laws pertaining to recording audio/video in your state. Make sure you Google something like "dash cam recording laws [your state]" in order to figure out what the rules are. In most cases, you will need to put up a small "you are on camera"-type sticker that can be acquired on Amazon.com.

Not only will a dash cam record things like accidents and incidents, it can prevent bad behavior. When passengers know they're on camera, they tend to be better behaved, and if you're ever having problems with a rider, you can always mention that they're being recorded.

I think a dash cam can also give peace of mind to your spouse or significant other. I know that when I first started driving for Uber and Lyft, my wife was a little worried about me driving a bunch of strangers around at night, but knowing that I had the dash cam definitely put her mind at ease.

What to do when sh&% hits the fan

A lot of bad rides can be avoided altogether with these strategies. But what if you've done everything right and you still run into a problematic passenger?

The most important thing you can do is try and defuse the situation. With every action you take, you'll want to think whether this is going to make things better or worse. And if you have the opportunity, a call to the police may be your best bet.

Since you're an independent contractor, you always have the right to cancel a ride if a passenger is making you feel unsafe or uncomfortable. But you'll want to be smart about it. It's probably not a good idea to kick a passenger out in a dark alley or on the side of the freeway.

Instead, head to a police station (again, this is where it pays to know your city's landmarks) or a well-lit gas station and explain to the passenger that you are no longer comfortable doing the ride. The passenger probably won't be happy, but at the end of the day, your safety is paramount. End the trip and report what happened to Uber via the driver app. You can report issues by going to the Help menu and selecting the trip you had an issue with, or by tapping on the phone icon to call Uber directly. Lyft has similar reporting procedures if you encounter a problem on their platform.

If it's a life-threatening issue, 911 is your best bet, but Uber does provide a critical response line that you can call in case you get into an accident or are having serious problems with a ride or passenger:

Uber Critical Safety Response Line: 1-800-285-6172

> **Pro-tip**: Save Uber's number in your phone right now so that you will have it in case of an emergency.

Lyft also has a critical response line[22] but you'll have to log on to your driver account at Lyft.com and go to the Help section in order to access it. We'll learn more about all the ways to contact Uber and Lyft in chapter 7.

In order to protect themselves, some drivers carry weapons, but it's important that you understand Uber's policy and, more importantly, your state and local laws. Uber's firearms policy[23] states that, "Uber prohibits riders and drivers

---

22   https://help.lyft.com/hc/en-us/articles/213584268-Report-an-accident-safety-incident-or-citation.
23   https://www.uber.com/legal/policies/firearms-prohibition-policy/en/.

from carrying firearms of any kind in a vehicle while using our app (to the extent permitted by applicable law). Anyone who violates this policy may lose access to Uber."

While Uber doesn't allow drivers to carry firearms, the law obviously supersedes Uber's rules, so understand that if you do carry a firearm while driving for Uber, you risk deactivation. But as one driver told me, "I'd rather get deactivated from Uber than deactivated from life."

Uber doesn't have a policy against nonlethal weapons like tasers and pepper spray, but the latter is not a good idea for an enclosed space like a car according to experts we've interviewed. I don't drive with a weapon of any kind, but I'm also above average in height and weight for a male, so it's rare that I feel unsafe.

Lyft's policy is more stringent and they don't allow for drivers or passengers to carry any types of weapons (lethal or nonlethal).

If you're not comfortable with this, start off by driving during the day and ease into things. Personally, I feel that driving for Uber and Lyft is safe but you have to know what you're doing. I use a two-way dash cam and establish from the get-go that I'm in charge—while still being as courteous as possible.

Handling lost or left behind items

When riders exit my vehicle at the end of a trip, I always do a quick scan of the backseat to make sure they didn't leave anything behind—phones are the most common lost item by far! But once in a while, I'll get a call from a passenger frantically asking me if they left their phone in my car. Uber passengers can contact you through a virtual phone number that Uber assigns if they report a lost item (so they won't have your personal cell phone number), but you can't contact them once a trip is over.

In some markets, Uber pays drivers for returning lost phones, but for the most part, you're on your own. How would you handle this situation? Below is how Uber driver and financial blogger Sam Dogen handles it:

Sam Dogen knows that people are tethered to their smartphones and that these phones are very important to them. But let's say you've dropped your rider off and are now on the other side of town when you get a phone call from your last passenger saying they left their phone behind.

You could drive all the way across town for the small fee Uber gives you, but time is money and if you're not driving passengers, you're not making money. Sam suggests telling passengers who've left behind valuables, "Hey, I'm at this location. Feel free to swing by and grab it, or alternatively, I can drop it off for you later for $20, $40." Whatever you think is fair payment for your time.

In this situation, you're not trying to rip anyone off. You're not trying to take advantage of someone because they left their phone in the car, but at the end of the day, Sam says that drivers should be compensated for their time. He's not going to drive one or two hours to return someone's phone because they left it in his car and not get any payment.

It may not surprise you that Sam is a retired Wall Street banker who now runs a personal finance blog called Financial Samurai.

You can listen to our interview with Sam about his driving experience at therideshareguy.com/episode37.

Service animals

It's against the law to refuse a ride to any passenger with a service animal, and Uber and Lyft are very strict about this policy. It doesn't matter if you don't like dogs, are allergic to dogs, or just don't want to do the ride; both companies have come under a lot of heat due to drivers refusing these requests and their policies have become much stricter.

You can ask a rider if their animal is a service dog or what duties has it been trained to do, but that's it. You can't ask for identification or for the rider to prove it's a service dog, so your best bet is to just accommodate these riders as the Americans with Disabilities Act (ADA) requires. I like to carry a towel in the trunk so that the dog can lie on the towel and not get hair everywhere.

Pro-tip: A towel also comes in handy for hairy passengers. Or riders who you pick up from the beach, pool party, etc.

Pukers

Uber and Lyft provide a safe way for people to imbibe and get a ride home, but sometimes we get passengers who have had way too much to drink. A lot of these riders just pass out in the backseat, but what happens if they puke in your car?

I try to avoid pukers at all costs but if it does happen, Uber and Lyft will charge the rider a cleanup fee that reflects the cost of cleaning. The fee is not meant to be punitive, nor is it meant to reflect the cost of downtime caused by the incident. It only exists to compensate you for the cost of cleaning.

That said, I allow people to eat in my car. But if they eat in my car and make a mess that I have to clean up? They're getting a cleaning fee. I don't warn them. I assume they're adults who understand not to trash someone else's property. If they've made a mess and clean it up themselves, no problem. If not, I'm taking pics and submitting them. You can ask Uber or Lyft for a cleaning fee by going to the Help menu in the driver app and reporting a problem with the trip. Then you can upload photos directly to your inquiry.

Cleanings fees range from $25 to $150 and the worse it looks, the more you get. So don't clean up anything until you take photos. For example, I made the mistake once of pulling out my removable rubber floor mats and taking a picture of them outside my car. Even though there was quite a lot there, my cleaning fee was less. I believe it was because Uber could see that I had removed them from my car, and was therefore easy to clean up.

Below are a few examples of cleaning fees drivers have received:

- Full-on puke: $150.
- Chocolate on the seat from a guy who ate a candy bar while drunk: $50.
- Guy who spilled his "dip" cup in my car and on the door (yuck!): $80.
- Drunk girl who ate two Taco Bell meals in under two miles and sounded like a ravenous dog: $30.

> **Pro-tip:** One thing to keep in mind is that if you report a puker to Uber and then give rides afterwards, Uber will not reimburse you for cleaning fees since, to them, it looks like the puke must not have been that bad if you were able to clean it (or not clean it!) and get back on the road. As we'll read below from Will, it's not that hard to clean puke yourself, so if you don't want a puker to end your night, you can always get your car cleaned and then switch to Lyft for the rest of the night in order to claim your cleaning fee from one company and continue earning with the other.

You get one chance at the cleaning fee. Uber and Lyft rarely increase the cleaning fee after they have decided what it should be. Once you submit your photos and they have decided on your fee, that's it.

In my first incident, for example, I didn't notice a significant amount of vomit in my doorjamb. It was actually the most voluminous part of what happened and could have increased my fee. I didn't see it until the next day because I was not thorough enough.

This means take your photos quickly, take a lot of them, and be very thorough. Digital photos are free, so get somewhere with good lighting and really look around. Look on the floor, the seat backs, the seat back pockets, the door panels, the ceiling, the doorjambs, the window and the opening the window goes into. Be *extremely* thorough. You don't want to miss out on part of the picture in your report, and you don't want to find dried puke the next day.

If you're going to drive during the party hours, drunks are part of the gig. This is a job, but it's also a public service. People need to know that if they call for a rideshare, it's going to show up, and if it shows up and they're drunk, it's not going to cancel on them.

The first thing I did as a driver was to purchase thirty emesis bags from Amazon. They have a nice hard round plastic ring to make it easy to hold on to when you're drunk and give you a better chance of being successful at its purpose.

And if you really want to be ready for pukers, you need to puke-proof your surfaces. Seat covers and floor mats will make cleaning a whole lot easier.

The first time someone puked in Will Preston's car, it cost him $140 to get it cleaned and Uber reimbursed him $150, but he lost a full night of driving. After that, Will was determined to puke-proof his car so that he could get back onto the road as quickly as possible in the event of a puker and still cash in on the puke fee given to him by Uber. Will found out the smelly way that being prepared for pukers can really add up, and in the course of a year of collecting puke fees, he netted over $1,500 in extra earnings.

Will puke-proofed his vehicle by getting seat covers and floor mats, and kept some basic cleaning supplies in the trunk. He did all he could to prevent pukers but he wasn't scared of them, either. When he did get a puker, he snapped photos, sent them off to Uber, cleaned everything up, and switched over to Lyft to keep on earning!

Most passengers are very pleasant

I've highlighted a lot of what can go wrong on a ride, but don't let that scare you. Most rides go off without a hitch and you'll probably find yourself enjoying the company of your passengers more than anything. Well, the ones who want to talk at least.

Below is a cool story about how one driver turned the monotony of driving into something more positive:

Rideshare driving can feel like a grind after a while, so it's important to keep things in context. John Ince, a Bay Area driver and frequent Rideshare Guy contributor, found this grind to really wear on him. As he pointed out, "Whenever something bad happens on a ride, it will be blamed on us, and we sometimes take a hit in ratings."

While he admitted it was easy to become jaded, he found one way to make rideshare driving infinitely more rewarding—for himself and his passengers. He bought a small "treasure chest" and put note cards and pens in it. From there, he encouraged passengers to write anything they wanted, secrets, drawings, notes for John himself, and leave it in the treasure chest.

It's been two years since he introduced the treasure chest, and he says the results have been intangible. "I've now accumulated hundreds of spontaneous, heartfelt, funny, profound personal notes from passengers. Whenever I get depressed about this gig, I pull them out and read a few. It never fails to lift my spirits. While I can't be sure, my intuition is telling me that the process of engaging passengers through this Treasure Chest/passenger notes idea has also boosted my ratings. It was not uncommon for passengers to tell me that this Treasure Chest is the best thing they've seen as a passenger and that I'm definitely getting five stars. Even if they're lying, it's been a lot of fun."

7

Where can I find driver support, community, and resources?

I GOT AN EMAIL ONE day from Uber saying that my insurance card was about to expire, so being the diligent driver that I am, I submitted my new insurance card. Unfortunately, Uber rejected my new insurance card because the starting date wasn't for another week. It turns out that there was no way to submit both cards at the same time and my account was temporarily deactivated!

After countless emails back and forth with Uber support, they could not even understand my predicament, so I turned to a local driver Facebook group. Dozens of other drivers chimed in that they had experienced the same problem and the work-around was to take a picture of both insurance cards and upload them at the same time. Not a huge hassle but it would have been nice to hear that from Uber!

For all the flexibility and independence that being a rideshare driver affords, it has always been challenging to get good support from Uber and Lyft. One of the most popular articles[24] on our blog for years focused solely on the best ways to get in contact with Uber.

Uber has improved their customer support in recent years but still has a ways to go. There are some topics that Uber isn't legally allowed to provide training on and there are others that they don't really talk about—like how to drive for Uber and Lyft at the same time. Lyft experiences many of the same customer support issues, and while some drivers prefer one company over the other, the only noticeable difference I've seen is that Uber has more options than Lyft because they're the bigger company.

Here in Los Angeles for example, Uber has fourteen Greenlight centers spread across the city, while Lyft has just one Hub in downtown.

Uber and Lyft will ultimately be the best point of contact for some of the more logistical issues (like getting your vehicle approved to drive), but some other resources are at your disposal. Unlike a traditional job where you get training and can talk to your coworker if any issues arise, with rideshare driving, you're on your own for the most part. It's up to you to seek out the information.

How to get in contact with Uber and Lyft

Uber used to be a difficult company to get hold of, but now they have a variety of options for drivers:

---

24   therideshareguy.com/top-6-ways-to-contact-uber-when-you-need-help/.

- Phone support 24/7: The phone number can be found in the Uber driver app under the Help section. Tap on the phone icon.
- In-App support: Open the Uber driver app and submit a ticket by going to the Help Section. You should get a response within twenty-four hours via email and/or through the app.
- In-person support: Uber operates dozens of Greenlight centers across the country where you can speak with knowledgeable representatives and troubleshoot certain issues more effectively. You can find the locations at help.Uber.com. Lyft also has started to open in-person "Hubs" across the country and the locations/times can be found on Lyft.com.

When contacting Uber and Lyft for help, it's important that you clearly describe your question and try to only ask one question at a time. Most of Uber's and Lyft's customer service representatives are not drivers, so they tend to provide better support on issues like troubleshooting, company policy, and requests.

Some customer service agents are more knowledgeable than others, so if you're not getting the help you need, try hanging up and calling again (or submitting a new request if you're doing it through the app). Although it can be frustrating at times dealing with customer support, as drivers we're also in the business of customer support, so do your best to be understanding and patient—as tough as it may seem.

Typically, in-app support is best suited for the simpler requests, and phone support and in-person help is better for the more complicated issues.

If you're the do-it-yourself type, Uber has an extensive

Help section on help.Uber.com where you can type in your city and find things like rates, rules, and regulations. A wealth of knowledge is on Uber's website and within the Help section of the driver app, but it may take some digging. Most of this content has been curated by employees at Uber's corporate offices so it tends to be a little better than the help you'd get through a customer service agent.

Lyft has similar in-app help resources, or you can turn to their website at help.Lyft.com.

If you find that you're not getting anywhere with Uber's or Lyft's agents, or not getting a response at all, one of the options that I like to turn to is social media. A lot of companies these days are putting their best and brightest customer service people on their social media team so you may be able to get better help there. I've had many issues resolved by tweeting Uber (twitter.com/uber_support) or Lyft (twitter.com/askLyft) or contacting them through their Facebook Page. You can either comment on one of their public posts or send them a message directly through their page under the "send a message" button (facebook.com/Uber or facebook.com/Lyft).

If you find that you need immediate police or medical attention, call 911. Once all parties are out of harm's way and the necessary authorities have been contacted, Uber does have a critical response line at 800-285-6172 if you need to speak with them.

Lyft also has a critical response line,[25] but you'll have to log on to your driver account at Lyft.com and go to the Help section in order to access it.

---

25 https://help.lyft.com/hc/en-us/articles/213584268-Report-an-accident-safety-incident-or-citation.

Below are some examples of the best support options for common problems you might face while driving:

- **Passenger throws up in your car:** Finish the ride, take a bunch of pictures, and report it to Uber or Lyft by going to the Help section in the driver app.
- **You get into an accident with another car:** If anyone is seriously injured, call 911 immediately. If no one is seriously injured, you can still call the police to take a report and then report the accident to Uber or Lyft using their critical response line.
- **Passenger forgets their phone in your car:** If you notice that a passenger left behind an item like a cell phone, report this to Uber or Lyft by navigating to the Help menu in the driver app and reporting a lost item. If you're not sure whose it is, wait for the passenger to report it missing and Lyft/Uber will reach out to you directly.
- **You're logged in to drive but not receiving requests:** For more complex issues like this, it's generally best to go in person to Uber's Greenlight Center or Lyft's Hub so they can help troubleshoot.
- **Questions about pay on a specific trip or promotion:** This is a tricky one, but if you encounter issues with payments, I'd start by submitting a request from the Help section of the driver app. If they're not able to solve it and you want to escalate, try heading to social media or going in person to a support center.

How to connect with other rideshare drivers

Ridesharing can be a lonely gig. Passengers are often absorbed in their phones or their own conversations, and other drivers are scattered across town, each in their own car. And since Uber and Lyft are app-based, there's no physical lounge area for drivers to socialize with one another. But there are some real benefits to hanging out with other drivers.

For new drivers, this is especially true. Spending time with other drivers lets you gather valuable insight into your local rideshare market since many aspects of ridesharing are unique to certain areas. For instance, local regulations regarding pickups and drop-offs at the airport vary wildly. Likewise, some lesser-known hotspots with lots of passengers may be in your city that you might not be aware of.

Veteran drivers can also recommend things like clean twenty-four-hour bathrooms, good spots for meals, and other local secrets that even the best rideshare book (this one!) might not be able to tell you.

The benefits don't stop there, whether you're a brand-new driver or a seasoned veteran. If you happen to talk shop with a fellow driver over lunch or dinner, you can deduct that meal as a business expense on your taxes (which we'll learn more about in chapter 8). Plus, being plugged in to your local rideshare community helps keep you informed of new developments in your market.

The easiest place to start is online since there's a wide array of driver groups on Facebook. Some are dedicated to drivers in a specific area, while others are more general. For a list of rideshare groups, head to therideshareguy.com/facebookgroups, or use Facebook's search bar to find out if there's one specific to your area. If not, why not start one? It's free, and it only takes a few minutes. If you advertise it well, it just might take off.

Facebook isn't the only way to stay in touch. For those of you who prefer to stay off the Facebook grid, there are a couple large forums for drivers:

Uber Drivers Subreddit

If you're not familiar with Reddit, it's essentially an online forum where users post text, links, and threaded replies. Then, other users vote on each piece of content that gets posted. Content with a lot of up-votes floats to the top, and content with a lot of down-votes sinks to the bottom. You filter what you see first by how many votes it has gotten in the last day, week, month, and so forth—or you can use the search bar to find answers to specific questions.

Find the Uber subreddit at reddit.com/r/uberdrivers, and don't forget about Lyft at reddit.com/r/lyftdrivers.

UberPeople

For a more traditional online forum, many drivers frequent UberPeople. This one has a pretty large user base as well, and posts are sorted into easy-to-follow categories, such as pay, technology, ratings, insurance, and so forth. To browse the forum, log on to UberPeople.net. Although the name might suggest it's only for Uber drivers, plenty of forums are dedicated to Lyft drivers on UberPeople.

Some of these online communities tend to be a bit negative but they contain a lot of good information. You just have to find the right group and/or group of people willing to help—or be willing to wade through the naysayers to get what you need.

While online options are great for communicating from home, it can also be nice to have a coworker to chat with during long waiting periods—or even to give real-time updates on road conditions or other happenings in your local area. For this, some drivers use walkie-talkie apps like Voxer and Zello to stay in touch on the road.

Popular Waiting Spots

If the technical approach is too daunting, there's a simpler way to connect: in person! Most cities have at least a couple spots where rideshare drivers are never in short supply—usually by popular bars or hotels, sports game/event parking lots, or especially in designated waiting areas at the airport. Strike up a conversation with fellow drivers who are hanging out there to exchange advice, or just funny passenger stories! In my experience, a driver is never short on those.

Of course, you always have the option of taking a ride as a passenger since that will allow you to see what it's like from the customer's perspective and talk to a driver.

Other In-Person Meetups

There aren't a ton of in-person events for rideshare drivers, but you may be able to find a few options. In most large cities, Uber has a dedicated support office. This is a great place to run into drivers and strike up a conversation. If you drive for Lyft, you might be aware that the company will occasionally organize local meetups for drivers to hang out and socialize. They usually publish these in their weekly Lyft update email, so be sure to keep an eye on that for any upcoming events.

In addition, you can even organize your own meetup and publicize it in your local Facebook group or forum. These mixers are a great way to connect and make friends with your coworkers and pick up some driving tips you might not have thought up yet.

The best online blogs and YouTubers to follow

I'm a little biased here since I run a blog, podcast, and You-Tube channel for rideshare drivers, but some of the best information you can get will come from rideshare blogs and You-Tube channels. Forums and Facebook groups can be tough to search and, as mentioned, there are a whole host of topics that the companies themselves don't cover, so in that case, you'll want to know where to get the best info for drivers.

Regarding blogs, below are a few top sites that you'll want to check out:

- TheRideshareGuy.com
  - ° This is my blog! Since 2014, we've published four posts a week that help rideshare drivers with everything from getting started and signed up, to what's going on in the industry, and tips and tricks for maximizing your income. All of our contributors are rideshare drivers and hail from all over the United States.
- MaximumRidesharingProfits.com
  - ° This is the video training course that we offer to new drivers, but there's also a handy blog where we transcribe our most popular YouTube videos and publish two posts a week.
- RidesharingDriver.com
  - ° Doug Herrera is an original Lyft driver out of

Orange County, California, and his site has been teaching drivers all about rideshare services from the get-go.

- Ridester.com
  - ° Brett Helling runs a series of rideshare websites that showcase the knowledge of rideshare drivers across the country.

On The Rideshare Guy, we publish four new articles every week and all of our writers are existing Uber and Lyft drivers from across the country. We try to keep drivers up-to-date on the latest news in the industry but also produce content that you can't find anywhere else.

And in case you didn't know, YouTube is actually the second-biggest search engine these days. The platform is very conducive to rideshare driving since you can easily watch a few short videos in your downtime between rides. A host of great YouTube vloggers are creating content for rideshare drivers, and I encourage you to check out the following:

- The Rideshare Guy - therideshareguy.com/youtube
  - ° My YouTube channel answers everything from situational questions like *what do I do if a passenger tries to bring a beer into my car* to app walkthroughs so you can be better prepared.
- Uber Man - therideshareguy.com/UberMan
  - ° Randy Shear, a.k.a. UberMan, was one of the first YouTube rideshare vloggers and has a loyal and dedicated following of drivers. Randy's videos cover rideshare topics but he also likes to keep you updated on everything that's going on in his life.

- The Simple Driver - therideshareguy.com/thesimpledriver
  - ° Calvin Hill is an Uber/Lyft driver based out of Atlanta, Georgia, and has some of the most in-depth videos on driving that you will find. Calvin is all about the entrepreneurial side of being a driver and his content will challenge you and get you thinking about ways to improve your business.
- Rideshare Professor - therideshareguy.com/rideshareprofessor
  - ° Torsten is an experienced Uber driver based out of Los Angeles, California, who provides all sorts of detailed advice but also has experience as an UberBlack and UberSelect driver.
- Jermaine Ellis - therideshareguy.com/Jermaine
  - ° Jermaine is a rideshare and delivery driver out of San Francisco, California, and is a prolific vlogger, often posting one video a day on a variety of topics related to the sharing economy.

One other content medium that you may want to check out is The Rideshare Guy Podcast, where we interview everyone from Uber and Lyft drivers to CEOs of start-ups and reporters covering the industry. Most podcasts are 30–45 minutes and you'll find a wide variety of stories, strategies, and ideas here: therideshareguy.com/itunes.

Jermaine Ellis is a popular rideshare YouTube vlogger (video blogger—and he also covers travel and food) who covers driving for Uber and Lyft online. Jermaine got started with rideshare driving and delivery for the same reasons many drivers get started: flexibility, quick pay, earning on your own time, and more.

He first started his YouTube channel to highlight his travels around the United States and his hometown of San Francisco, but then branched out into covering rideshare and delivery for new drivers. At one point, he was making daily vlogs for his subscribers and is one of the most authentic personalities in the industry. He now earns a full-time living from his YouTube channel off a mix of affiliate advertising and referrals.

8

What does it take to be an independent contractor? (Including taxes!)

WHEN I FIRST STARTED DRIVING, I was only looking to make a few hundred bucks a week, but what I didn't realize is that I was now running a business. And unlike a regular W-2 job, Uber and Lyft don't take money out of your paycheck for taxes so it's up to you to put some money aside.

It isn't all doom and gloom though—there's some extra work you'll have to do as an independent contractor and newly minted business owner, but that's one of the trade-offs for being your own boss and working whenever you want. If you know what you're doing, you could end up paying next to nothing in taxes because of all the deductions you now have access to.

Managing your hours

Driving for Uber and Lyft is unlike any job you've ever done, but like other jobs, there are both positives and negatives. I love being able to set my own schedule and work when and where I want, but as this chapter has shown, there are some extra considerations that you also need to worry about.

At a normal W-2 job, your employer will take care of taxes, expenses, and provide you with resources to improve your skills and keep you happy. As a rideshare driver, this responsibility is now on you. Purchasing this book is a great way to step up the education piece but it will also be on you to make sure you don't overdo it. You don't have a boss who will say, "You look tired; maybe you should take a break." And if you want to take a vacation, you're going to have to plan for it and save accordingly because there's no paid vacation time, sick leave, or unemployment when driving for Uber.

I've always been a part-time driver, so I've never put in more than about twenty to thirty hours a week, but it's important for you to find your limit. I don't know if I could do forty to fifty hours a week because then it would feel too much like a regular job. While not everyone has that choice, it's important to pace yourself. Find the most profitable times to work that align well with your schedule and that way you can work smarter, not harder.

Being a rideshare driver also isn't the healthiest of professions. I don't know about you, but I get hungry when I drive. That is a great combination for gaining weight.

When you're driving, it's important that you take breaks whenever possible and get out of the car, stretch, maybe even walk around. Sometimes I'll even get out to open the doors for my riders, but that is tougher when it's busy. Some drivers make fun of me for doing this, but it's a small thing to do to get the blood flowing and to provide an experience that is above and beyond what other drivers are doing.

It's important that you keep your health in mind because it will affect your driving habits. If you're not getting enough sleep and you go out driving, not only is this bad for your health, but it could also put you at a higher chance of getting into an accident.

Understanding your income and your expenses

It's easy to get caught up with how much you're earning as an Uber and Lyft driver, but one thing you have to realize is that as an independent contractor, you're also responsible for all of your expenses. Since it can be tricky to calculate some of your expenses, a lot of drivers opt to just skip that part. But that's not a recipe for long-term success.

If you're rolling your eyes right now, I don't blame you. The nice thing is that you don't need to worry about your expenses right off the bat. During your first few months as a driver, it's more about learning the system, finding the best times to drive, and focusing on maximizing your income potential. Once you get the hang of things, you'll start to notice that those oil changes are coming up more frequently and the cost of new brakes will be something you need to budget for.

As a driver, your main expenses are going to revolve around vehicle use. A full-time driver will put around a thousand miles a week on their car, so in the short term, gas will be your number one expense.

Below is a typical earning situation based off real-life numbers and assuming a gas cost of $3 per gallon.

Miles Driven	1,000
Total Earnings	$1,100
Gas Cost (25 MPG)	$120
Net Earnings	$980

This analysis assumes that your car gets 25 miles per gallon (MPG), but that number will obviously vary. I guess there's a reason why the most popular rideshare vehicle in our most recent survey[26] was a Toyota Prius—gas mileage is super important to drivers.

Beyond gas, other expenses you'll need to consider regarding your vehicle are depreciation, insurance, and maintenance/repairs. You may not have the time to calculate this number for your vehicle but a good range of the cost to operate your vehicle is $0.20–$0.40 per mile.

Pro-tip: We've got a handy spreadsheet on our website to calculate the cost per mile for your vehicle: www.therideshareguy.com/CPM.

---

26   therideshareguy.com/rsg-2017-survey-results-driver-earnings-satisfaction-and-demographics/.

If you got a great deal on a two-year-old used Prius like Rideshare Guy contributor Will Preston, the cost per mile of operating your 2013 Prius will be just $0.195 per mile, which includes depreciation, cost of gas, and maintenance/repairs.[27]

On the other hand, if you drive a brand-new SUV that gets lower MPG and has a high interest rate, you could easily be closer to $0.40 per mile. The important thing to consider is that for every mile you drive, a cost is going to count against your income.

Drivers are only paid for miles when they have a passenger in the car (Uber is testing payouts for extra-long pickups). So for every mile you drive without a passenger, you're losing money.

While your vehicle is going to be your biggest expense, another item to consider is taxes. Since drivers are independent contractors, they'll have to pay the self-employment tax plus federal and state taxes on any income. We'll go into more detail on this in a few pages, but if you do a good job of tracking all your deductions, your taxable income could be negligible and this won't be much of an issue.

In some jurisdictions, drivers are required to take classes, get business licenses, and more, but for the most part, these expenses are nominal and limited to just a few cities. Find out about your city's local regulations to become a rideshare driver on Uber's website as outlined in chapter 7.

---

27   http://therideshareguy.com/how-to-calculate-per-mile-earnings-instead-of-per-hour/.

Accounting software, tips, and tricks

Tracking all of your income and expenses can be as difficult or as easy as you'd like it to be, but the important thing is that you do it. Even if you're only thinking about it on a weekly basis, it's important to understand that for every dollar you make as a driver, a certain cost went into making that dollar.

Personally, I find that using simple spreadsheets, apps, and software makes the process a lot easier. And it also allows you to see trends over time so that you can make informed business decisions just like a real business owner would do.

Joe Starzyk is a licensed CPA and specializes in helping rideshare drivers with their taxes. According to Joe, the standard mileage rate is often easier and more tax beneficial for rideshare drivers. You don't have to worry about tracking every little expense. You don't have to worry about figuring out depreciation. And barring any extraordinary circumstances, rideshare drivers using a relatively fuel-efficient vehicle will have a higher tax deduction using the standard mileage rate.

When it comes to documentation, Joe says that you can make tax time easier for yourself by keeping track of your expenses and mileage throughout the year. Don't wait until tax time to try and put everything together. For many drivers, a simple Excel spreadsheet will suffice, and take pictures of receipts so you don't have to worry about losing them. Pictures of receipts are perfectly acceptable to maintain in your tax records.

If you are using an app to maintain a mileage log, use the app to track your expenses to keep things simple, if you can.

Drivers often assume everything you need to prepare your tax return is included on the Form 1099. This is not true. More items are needed to prepare a complete and accurate tax return.

As we touched on in chapter 2, one of the most important things you can do for your business is to track your mileage.

Uber provides the total number of miles you drove while online in your 1099-K summary that you'll receive in January for the year prior. You can find this information by logging on to partners.Uber.com and navigate to the tax section.

Lyft also provides your total number of miles while you were online and their tax summary can be found on Lyft.com under the tax section of your dashboard.

If you forgot to track your mileage, you can go off of the numbers provided by Uber and Lyft, but it won't include all of your deductible miles. So it's important to keep your own logs to maximize your deduction. There are a whole host of mileage tracking options, but the two options I use personally and recommend to drivers are Stride Drive and Quickbooks Self-Employed.

Stride Drive is a free mileage tracking app for Android and iOS that allows you to automatically record all of your mileage and expenses. Some drivers like to record their odometer manually or use a spreadsheet, but I like Stride Drive because it's all done for you and it prints out a handy report that you can input into your tax software or give to your CPA at the end of the year.

QBSE is another popular option among drivers, and while it is a paid service, the cost is nominal and in addition to mileage tracking, it allows you to see a more holistic view of your finances. At any time, you can run a report on your driving history and see how your income stacks up against your expenses for the previous month, previous quarter, or even the previous year. It also allows you to calculate your estimated quarterly taxes. The app integrates with TurboTax, so come tax time, you can easily import all of your information and file your taxes.

Pro-tip: You can find a full list of mileage tracking apps at therideshareguy.com/mileageapps.

The three most important rules when dealing with the IRS are documentation, documentation, and documentation. I use my QBSE app to track the starting mileage every time I leave the house to rideshare drive and the ending mileage every time I arrive home. If you didn't keep this type of detailed records, then your next best bet is to use the mileage totals from Uber and Lyft or try to calculate it using an alternative method.[28]

A full-time rideshare driver will easily put a thousand miles a week on their car, which translates into a $535 deduction each week or $27,820 through the year (which is pretty massive).

---

28 http://therideshareguy.com/what-can-drivers-do-if-they-forgot-to-track-their-mileage/.

Some confusion arises around which miles you can deduct as a driver since some CPAs will tell you that you can only deduct miles while you're logged on to the driver app. But personally, I deduct all the miles from the second I leave my house until I arrive home.

It's up to you and/or your CPA on how aggressive you want to be, but if you use Uber's or Lyft's destination filter at the beginning or end of your shift, I think that makes an even stronger case that those miles are deductible.

Getting your rideshare taxes done right

One of the things a lot of new drivers overlook when they're just getting started is taxes. Taxes as an independent contractor might seem scary, but they're actually pretty simple.

Every year in late January or early February, Uber and Lyft send out 1099s for the prior tax year that detail how much you made, what fees they took out, and the miles you drove. Since drivers are independent contractors, all that means for your taxes is that you'll have to file a Schedule C in addition to your regular 1040.

Dealing with 1099s: 1099-K vs 1099-Misc

Uber and Lyft both consider themselves *third-party payment processors*. I was familiar with that term because I used to accept PayPal payments with one of my old businesses, and I would only receive a 1099-K in years where I made over $20,000 and did two hundred transactions.

A third-party payment processor is a company that facilitates payments between consumers and business owners.

That's why you see companies like PayPal, Amazon Payments, and Square label themselves as third-party payment processors.

Now obviously Lyft and Uber do a whole lot more than facilitate payments, but this is the distinction they've decided to go with. This won't affect the amount you pay in taxes, but it does mean they'll report gross income, and you will have to subtract the fees/commissions they charge.

Uber's 1099s

Uber only sends out 1099-Ks to drivers who did more than 200 rides and made more than $20,000. But even though, you may not receive a 1099-K from Uber, you'll still have to pay taxes on your earnings.

If you made over $600 in referral bonuses or miscellaneous income, then you will also receive a 1099-MISC. The 1099-MISC is pretty straightforward: the amount on the form is what you made and will be combined with the gross fares from your 1099-K.

Where it gets confusing is with the 1099-K, since Uber reports gross fares including all of their fees, tolls, fuel card, etc. All you need to do is combine the number on your 1099-K and/or 1099-MISC. That is the total that will go down as your income on your Schedule C.

I know what you're thinking. That number is a lot higher than what you actually made—and you're 100 percent right. In order to get your true earnings, you will now have to sum up the expenses from your 1099 Summary Page.[29] Your 1099 Summary Page can be accessed by logging in to your driver account on partners.Uber.com and navigating to the Tax Information section.

---

29   https://partners.uber.com/p3/tax-compliance/forms

Driver Partner | Uber   https://partners.uber.com/statements/tax-summary/

NOT AN OFFICIAL 1099 FORM

U B E R

2014 TAX SUMMARY JOHN SMITH

Many of the items listed below may be deductible, please consult with a
tax expert for more guidance.

1099-K BREAKDOWN   **1099-MISC BREAKDOWN**

Gross Fares (Uber Fee included)[1] ......$1,083.06   Referrals..$1,169.00

Tolls...................................$36.70   **TOTAL**.......................$1,169.00

Split Fare Fee..........................$0.50

Safe Rides Fee.........................$45.00   **OTHER ITEMS**

TOTAL...........................$1,165.26   Device Subscription.................$40.00

                                                      Uber Fee................................$190.69

                                                      On-Trip Mileage[2] ....332.5 miles

[1]Gross fares are calculated as base + time + distance (this
includes the Uber Fee)

[2]On-trip mileage only. Additional mileage may be deductible.

Items in **bold** may be deductible. Check with a tax
professional to learn more.

> This number ties to the total on the 1099-K. Record this as an earning on your Schedule C.

> This number ties to the total on the 1099-MISC. Record this as an earning on your Schedule C.

> These numbers relate to expenses that Uber took out before they paid you. The ones under the 1099-K will be included as both an earning and an expense. The ones under "Other Items" will be included as an expense. Record both under the "Commissions and Fees" (Line 10) on the Schedule C.

> This number relates to mileage. Uber did not make any deductions for it, and thus it has no effect on the total for the 1099-K or 1099-MISC, or how much they paid to your bank account. However, this is an expense you can write off for your "driving services business".

Tolls, split fare fees, and safe ride fees will be listed as both earnings and expenses. Since they are already included in the income portion of your Schedule C, you will combine them with the Uber fee in order to get your total expenses. That number will be entered on line 10 of your Schedule C (Commissions and fees).

If you'd like to do one final sanity check, you can easily add up all of your payouts from your partner statements throughout the year, and that number should equal your [Total Income (1099-K gross fares + 1099-MISC)] − [Commission and fees (all of Uber's fees listed on the 1099-K Summary)].

You may be tempted to just enter the sum of your partner payment statements on your Schedule C as your total income. While this would produce the same final net profit, it could cause a mismatch with the number Uber reports to the IRS as your total income, so that method is not advised.

Lyft's 1099s

In the past, Lyft handled their 1099-MISC the exact same way as Uber: drivers who earned over $600 in bonuses, mentor rides, etc., receive one. But starting in 2016, they've changed their 1099-K rules and now send a 1099-K to all drivers who earned at least $600 in gross ride receipts. If you did not meet that threshold, you will not receive a 1099-K.

Remember, regardless of whether you get a 1099 or not, you still have to pay taxes on all the money you earned. In order to correctly report your income, you'll need to head over to Lyft's tax summary page on Lyft.com. There you'll see your gross ride earnings, Lyft commission, and tolls paid. Note that Lyft does not include the trust and safety fee like Uber so you can ignore this number completely.

Lyft Gross Ride Earnings Example:

Gross ride earnings	$157.83
Lyft commission	-($8.97)
Tolls paid	-$0.00
Net ride earnings	$148.86

The process is pretty simple from this point on since you will take your gross ride earnings and add that to your 1099-MISC earnings (if you received one) and enter that as income on your Schedule C. Add up Lyft's commission and tolls paid and enter that in line 10 of your Schedule C (Commission and fees).

Tax advice for drivers who work for both Uber and Lyft

If you follow our advice, you'll probably end up with multiple 1099s from Uber and Lyft. If that's the case, you still only have to file one Schedule C, but you will need to combine the income from Lyft and Uber on your Schedule C and combine the commission and fees from Lyft and Uber. Make sure you account for the correct expenses as detailed above.

Since Uber and Lyft are both considered the same type of "rideshare driving business," you only need to fill out one Schedule C. If you also did delivery, technically you're supposed to do a separate Schedule C, but that's a bit of a gray area. You could probably argue that since Uber now offers UberEats, for example, your business is really more providing "logistic services" than rideshare or delivery type services.

Mileage deduction

There are two ways to deduct your mileage: the standard mileage rate and the actual expenses method. For most drivers, the standard mileage rate will likely make more financial sense, and it will be a lot easier. Note that if you opt for the standard mileage rate, you must choose to use that in the first year the car is used as a business. In later years, you can then choose either the standard mileage rate or the actual expenses method.

If you choose the standard mileage rate, you cannot deduct actual car operating expenses. That means you won't be able to deduct maintenance and repairs, gas, oil changes, insurance, and registration fees. The standard mileage rate includes all these items, as well as depreciation.

For 2017, the standard mileage rate was 53.5 cents per mile. That basically includes all the costs to operate your vehicle: gas, depreciation, oil changes, maintenance, repairs, etc.

Remember, the actual cost to own and operate your vehicle is not 53.5 cents per mile. That is the deduction amount you will get from the IRS. Your actual cost should be a whole lot less as we touched on in chapter 9, especially if you want to be profitable as a rideshare driver.

Actual Expenses Method

Instead of using the standard mileage rate, you can alternatively deduct the actual cost of using your car for business, plus depreciation. This requires a lot more record keeping, but it can result in a bigger deduction. If you decide to use this method, you must keep careful track of all the costs incurred for your car during the year, including items such as the following:

- gas and oil changes
- repairs and maintenance
- depreciation of your original vehicle and improvements
- car repair tools
- license fees
- parking fees for business trips
- registration fees
- tires
- insurance

- car washing
- lease payments
- towing charges

If you're not sure about the standard mileage rate versus actual vehicle expenses, it's a good idea to use the former the first year you use the car for business. This leaves all your options open for later years.

Standard Mileage Rate vs. Actual Expenses Method

In general, rideshare drivers will be better off using the standard mileage rate if you drive a smaller car. Since you get the same fixed deduction rate no matter how much the car is worth, this option works best for drivers with inexpensive and/or fuel-efficient vehicles.

The actual expense method usually provides a larger deduction if you drive a larger, more expensive car or an SUV or minivan. The fewer business miles you drive, the better off you'll be with the actual expense method.

Yet, the only way to know for sure which option is best for you is to keep careful track of your costs the first year you use your car for business. Another reason I like QBSE is because it allows you to run the numbers and determine if your deduction will be larger using the standard mileage rate or actual expense method.

Remember, if you don't use the standard mileage rate in the first year of business, you can't use it again in the future. If you use the standard mileage rate the first year, you can switch to the actual expense method in a later year. Then, you can switch back and forth between the two methods after that, with a few restrictions.

If you're leasing a vehicle, you are allowed to deduct miles. But if you use the standard mileage rate for the first year, you must use it for the entire remainder of the lease period.

Other deductions

Deductions are a business owner's best friend, and if you're creative, you should be able to significantly reduce your taxable income. Expenses like car washes, cell phone use, candy/water/etc., Spotify membership, Bluetooth, trunk organizers, and anything used for rideshare purposes may be deductible as long as they are "ordinary and necessary."[30]

The only thing you'll need to watch out for regarding deductions is with items like a cell phone that may be used for both personal and business use. Generally, you will need to allocate between personal and business use, so if you use the phone 50 percent of the time for business and 50 percent of the time for personal, you would only be able to deduct half of the cost of the phone and monthly subscription.

> **Pro-tip**: Look for items that can be used both personally and for business. For example, if you like to travel and record footage with a GoPro, that same GoPro could double as a dash cam when you're driving for Uber. If you use the GoPro 90 percent of the time for business, you would get to deduct 90 percent of its cost.

---

30   http://www.irs.gov/Businesses/Small-Businesses-&-Self-Employed/Deducting-Business-Expenses.

How most drivers file their taxes

A majority of drivers file their taxes using online software like TurboTax but about 30 percent use a CPA. If you're going to go the CPA route, I recommend you find someone who's knowledgeable in small business and/or rideshare drivers. There are millions of rideshare drivers these days, so it shouldn't be too hard to find a CPA who is familiar with Uber, but you can always reach out to me directly if you need a recommendation.

How do you file your taxes every year?

1,150 responses

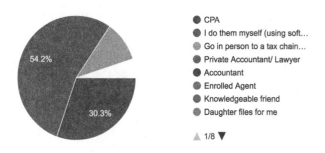

Legend:
- CPA
- I do them myself (using soft...
- Go in person to a tax chain...
- Private Accountant/ Lawyer
- Accountant
- Enrolled Agent
- Knowledgeable friend
- Daughter files for me

▲ 1/8 ▼

Estimated taxes

If you're a W-2 employee, your employer withholds taxes from every paycheck and sends the money to the IRS. That way, you pay your income taxes as you go and may even get a nice refund come tax time. But if you are a self-employed rideshare driver, you may need to pay estimated taxes each quarter. So how much should you pay?

If you'll owe less than $1,000 in taxes at the end of the year, you won't need to pay estimated taxes. For most everyone else, you're going to need to pay taxes as you go.

If you work a regular W-2 job in addition to rideshare driving, one way to avoid paying estimated taxes is to increase your withholding amount for your regular job. This means you'll pay more in taxes on your W-2 income, but come tax time, that will count against the taxes you would have owed from rideshare driving.

For others though, you'll need to make quarterly estimated tax payments four times a year.

Frequently asked rideshare tax questions

Why is the amount on my 1099-K from Uber higher than what I earned last year?
Since Uber considers themselves a third-party payment processor, the amount shown on your 1099-K will include the amount you earned plus Uber's commission, tolls, etc. It's up to you to subtract the fees and tolls using the example above.

Why didn't Lyft send me a 1099?
If you made less than $600, you won't receive a 1099-K from Lyft. You still need to pay taxes on the money you made, so head to your Lyft summary page and get the info you need to do your taxes.

What is the business code for Uber and Lyft for my Schedule C?
For Uber & Lyft use: 485300 Taxi & Limousine Service. Business codes are used by the IRS to categorize your business for statistical purposes only. The code you enter will not affect the outcome of your tax return.

What if I'm renting a car to drive for Uber or Lyft?
If you're renting a car from a program like Lyft's Express Drive, then you cannot take the standard mileage deduction. Instead, deduct your weekly rental payments and allocate your percentage of personal and business use (you'll need to track your miles in order to be able to do this).

Why did I get two 1099-K's from Uber?
Some drivers have received two 1099-K's in the past and if that's the case, you'll need to combine the income from both and add it to your Schedule C.

9

How can you diversify your rideshare income?

You're a rideshare pro now. You're a five-star driver, you're maximizing your income, and you know how to handle any situation a ride throws at you. But driving for Uber and Lyft can provide even more business opportunities that you'll want to take advantage of.

It only took about a week of rideshare driving for me to realize the need for content regarding what it was like to be a driver. At the time, a bunch of Facebook groups and a couple forums with drivers asking questions were available, but I noticed that everyone was asking the same thing. New drivers didn't have any authoritative resources.

As I gained more experience, I started blogging on The Rideshare Guy about what it was like to be a driver and mentoring new drivers. This quickly developed into a thriving business and, in 2015, I eventually left my full-time job as an engineer to become a full-time rideshare blogger.

Being an Uber or Lyft driver is a great job for a lot of people, but there are also many ways to leverage your driving experience and diversify your income. I was able to build a business around helping drivers, but that's not the only way to do it.

Taking your game to the next level

It doesn't take long for the average driver to start peeking at the rate cards for the higher-level services like UberSELECT and UberXL and get just a little jealous. Here in Los Angeles for example, UberSELECT pays drivers about two to three times more than UberX.[31]

25% Commission	UberSELECT	UberX
Base Fare	$3.75	$0.00
Per Mile	$1.76	$0.68
Per Minute	$0.30	$0.11
Per-Minute Wait Time	$0.30	$0.11
Minimum Trip Earnings	$6.75	$2.63
Cancellation Fee	$7.50	$3.75

The big caveat with driving for UberSELECT is that in order to be eligible for these trips, you'll need a premium vehicle like a Lexus or BMW sedan, and obviously these cars cost a lot more to purchase, and thus the higher rates.

A lot of drivers ask me if driving for UberSELECT is worth it. It mostly depends on your city and driving habits.

---

31   As of 9/7/2017.

The typical UberSELECT passenger is someone who values a nicer car and experience, so think business passengers, a couple on a nice date, or similar situations.

You probably won't get many Select rides on a Friday night at 1 a.m., but if you like driving Friday and Saturday evenings from around 6 to 10 p.m., that could line up well with times of peak demand for UberSELECT. You won't be nearly as busy with UberSELECT, but for a lot of drivers that might be a good thing. If you can find something productive to do in your downtime, not having as many rides isn't a big deal.

Lyft has a similar service called Lyft Premier that features high-end vehicles as well. It's not as busy as UberSELECT but it can't hurt to add it as an option and maximize your chances of getting a request.

What about UberXL?

I think UberXL presents the best opportunity for drivers looking to upgrade since there's a lot of demand from the party hours crowd but also from families on vacation or groups with lots of luggage. XL vehicles are required to have six seat belts in addition to the driver, and while the rides pay drivers more than UberX rides, a minivan typically isn't a whole lot more expensive than a regular car. For a lot of drivers with large families, this could be the impetus you need to upgrade your vehicle and serve your family's needs at the same time.

As an XL driver, you have the option to accept UberXL and UberX rides or just UberXL rides. When it's busy, you'll be best suited sticking with XL only; but if UberX starts surging, it would make sense to be available for UberX rides too, since the surge could make up the difference.

Lyft has a similar service called Lyft Plus and the requirements and rates are nearly identical to Uber.

Driving for Uber's commercial platforms

Uber started as a black car–only service in San Francisco but these days, most of the company's business occurs on the UberX platform. UberBLACK and UberSUV rates are four to five times higher than UberX rates, but most commercial Uber drivers have a completely different setup from your typical UberX driver. Below is a list of all Uber's commercial offerings:

- **UberBLACK:** UberBLACK is the original Uber service that caters to high-end clients. These drivers are required to carry commercial insurance and maintain taxi licensing.
- **UberSUV:** UberSUV has all the same requirements as UberBLACK but drivers need an SUV capable of handling groups of six passengers or more.
- **UberLUX:** UberLUX is Uber's latest addition to the fleet. In addition to the extra insurance/licensing requirements, drivers also need a top-of-the-line luxury vehicle like a Tesla or BMW 7 series.

Torsten Kunert is a popular rideshare driver with his own YouTube channel called The Rideshare Professor. He initially started with UberX but has since moved into the UberBlack, Luxury, and SUV categories after quickly realizing that he could upgrade to owning a fleet of cars and focus on the luxury market.

Torsten drives in Los Angeles in an area with lots of celebrities (and wannabe celebrities), so he's found that a lot of passengers are looking for high-quality rides in luxury vehicles. Torsten was able to leverage this demand by creating an Executive Limo Service and buying SUVs at auctions to lease out.

Torsten has moved from being a rideshare driver (although he still drives and answers questions on his YouTube channel) to being a fleet owner, and he says his secret to success was marketing and promoting his cars through social media.

UberBLACK and UberSUV require drivers to maintain commercial insurance and special licensing in order to operate. Additionally, UberBLACK is closed off to individual drivers in almost every market so the only way to currently get onto UberBLACK is through a fleet owner. A fleet owner is a private individual whose fleet is anywhere from one to dozens of vehicles that are rented to drivers looking to work for UberBLACK. As a driver and renter, you pay a weekly fee (usually in the neighborhood of $500) to rent the car. You're responsible for all gas, while the fleet owner covers everything else: insurance, licensing, maintenance, and more.

Even though you may be able to earn higher rates as an UberBLACK or UberSUV driver, profits and flexibility will be limited due to the weekly rental fee.

One way to get around the UberBLACK requirement is to sign up for UberLUX. UberLUX requires drivers to have commercial insurance and special licensing, but they'll also need an ultra-premium vehicle like a Tesla or Range Rover. Since most of us probably don't have $100,000+ lying around, this isn't a realistic option, but I do know of drivers who had a Tesla and wanted to give Uber driving a shot and this would be one way to do it. I wouldn't recommend it if you're trying to maximize your income and minimize your risk since the service is such a niche product.

Earning driver and passenger referral bonuses

I've worked all sorts of different jobs in my life, but it wasn't until I started driving for Uber and Lyft that I got my first ever sign-up bonus. I always thought that sign-up bonuses were reserved for professional athletes, tech workers, and in-demand executives, but apparently rideshare drivers can get them too!

And once you become a driver, you'll be able to refer other drivers to the platform and earn money once they hit a certain trip threshold (for example, $200 after they take fifty trips). Uber and Lyft both provide links and referral codes to existing drivers. If you have friends who you think would benefit from the gig, it can pay to refer them.

Referral bonuses have decreased over time, but since the market for new drivers is so competitive, it isn't unheard of to see referral bonuses for as much as $500 in some of the top Uber and Lyft cities.

Some drivers complain that referring other drivers creates more competition, but I've never bought that argument. Uber and Lyft have certain targets for driver numbers in each city and if they can't get them from referrals, they'll just spend that money on other marketing efforts.

It's important to note that I'm a little biased here since one of our main sources of revenue on the blog comes from driver referrals. But I've also never been the type to shy away from competition. In fact, the reason why I am so open with my readers and share many strategies in this book is because I believe that teaching others only reinforces those principles in yourself and makes you a better driver.

Although passenger referral bonuses aren't as lucrative, if you do come across someone who's interested in signing up as a passenger, it can't hurt to share your code with them. Uber and Lyft both pay $5–10 to drivers who refer new passengers, and the passenger will typically get $10–$50 off their first ride depending on the city.

And if you're real slick, you'll keep a stack of Lyft passenger referral cards on hand while you're driving for Uber and vice versa. Uber usually surges higher than Lyft (Prime Time equivalent), so if you ever get an Uber ride on surge, that's a good time to tell passengers that they can get a free ride or two when they sign up for Lyft and then hand out your referral cards. Here is the link for the premium business cards that I personally use: therideshareguy.com/palm1.

Third-party companies that help drivers earn more

As the number of rideshare drivers in the United States has grown into the millions, we've started to see more and more companies offering products and services to drivers. At the start, there were a lot of services like Stride Drive and Quickbooks Self-Employed that helped drivers save money on taxes and with mileage tracking, but now we're seeing apps like Mystro and Cargo that actually aim to help drivers earn more money.

What is Mystro?

One of my favorite new start-ups looking to help drivers is called Mystro. As we touched on earlier, they aim to automate the process of driving for both Uber and Lyft. Savvy drivers know that when demand is slow, it pays to go online with both Uber and Lyft in order to increase your chances of getting a request.

In the past, this process was burdensome and very unsafe since you had to physically go online with the first app, then go online with the second app, and once you got a request, you had to accept it and then log off the other app before you got a new trip. Sometimes you got another request before you could log off the second app. Huge pain in the butt! Luckily, Mystro does all of this automatically for you.

Mystro was founded by an Uber and Lyft driver named Herb Coakley who's gotten over ten thousand rides under his belt. The app is available to drivers all over the world but it is not a rideshare company. The Mystro app interfaces with the Uber and Lyft driver apps in order to sign you on and off and accept or ignore trips on the driver's behalf. The app is currently only available for Android users, but I'm told an iOS version is in the works.

Mystro helps drivers get more trips, which allows them to make more money during slow times and to be picky with the rides that they'll accept during busy times. I like to filter for ETAs that are five minutes or less; if it's really busy, I'll drop the ETA down to three minutes. You'd be surprised by how easily you can get a seven- to eight-minute ETA request followed by a two-minute ETA request since so many riders are requesting rides during specific busy times and places. And since you're not paid for the distance/time to a rider, you'll always want to be conscious of those numbers and look to minimize them. In smaller cities where it's not as busy, use the same strategy but at higher ETA levels (ignore the fifteen-minute ETA requests, but take the seven-to eight-minute requests).

Another area where Mystro excels is safety. If you're driving around without Mystro and you get a trip request, you have to physically look at the screen on your phone and tap it to accept. Mystro automates the acceptance process and if you're doing Uber and Lyft at the same time, it eliminates the need to stare at your screen.

What is Cargo?

Cargo is a start-up based out of New York that provides drivers with a vending machine-box full of snacks and supplies for passengers (many of which are free). Drivers earn money from whatever is sold or given away through the Cargo box.

Cargo advertises that drivers can make an extra $150 per month with the Cargo box, which seems reasonable from my initial testing, but your results will vary. According to Cargo, earnings can vary between $120–305 per month for drivers, Cargo is only in limited markets right now.

Cargo probably won't double your income, but it could give it a nice boost since a lot of times intoxicated passengers are more than happy to pay a couple dollars for a bag of Skittles!

Other money-making opportunities for drivers

There's no shortage of companies looking to launch products and services for drivers, but I can tell you from working with many of them that it's a long road. It's easy to come up with a name and slap a landing page on a website, but developing, launching, and marketing a product to drivers across the country is a big challenge.

During your time as a rideshare driver, you'll probably encounter lots of these companies and it's important to evaluate each one on its cost, potential, and hassle factor. I'd be wary of any company that doesn't have a solid track record and good refund and return policies if it costs money.

Below are some other unique ways drivers have made money:

- In-vehicle video ads: Companies like Go Vugo have been around for a couple years but haven't quite gained a foothold with the driver community. I think there's a lot of potential here so it's an area to keep an eye on.
- Vehicle ads: Wrapify is a company that will pay rideshare drivers to wrap their vehicles in advertisements.
- Selling your own products: A lot of drivers have side hustles, so it's no surprise that many of them push their own products or services to passengers. If you're going to go this route, make sure that you're not too pushy or over the top. Only sell to those who want to be sold to.

Networking is the name of the game

After a while, you may find that you're meeting tons of interesting people and may even want to stay in contact with some of them. I like to keep things professional but there are countless opportunities for networking if that's what you're after.

Try to take advantage of the opportunities that come your way. Below are a few examples of how drivers have benefited from networking:

- Free law advice: A driver once told me a story about how he had a high-priced lawyer in the back of his car during a time when he was going through a legal issue. After a few minutes of friendly conversation, the lawyer was happy to provide legal advice for this driver for the rest of the ride!
- New employment opportunities: A San Francisco driver looking for a programming job told me that he would hang out around the top ten tech companies after working hours and try to give rides to people at the company. Eventually, he found one willing to make an introduction to a recruiter and he got the job!
- Love connections: I have a friend in Toronto that met his girlfriend while driving for Uber. While you have to remember that passengers are your customers, sometimes you can't help feeling a strong connection.

Rideshare driving can also open up possibilities to funding a new start-up as Mystro founder Herb Coakley discovered. As a driver, Herb thought it was unsafe that drivers had to switch between Uber and Lyft to pick up passengers and knew there had to be a better way.

He moved to San Francisco to pursue his idea. One day while driving rideshare, he pitched one of his passengers on the idea. The passenger turned out to be an investor, loved the idea, and ended up funding part of Mystro's seed round.

Listen to our interview with Herb at theridesshareguy.com/episode57.

How to respectfully push your side hustle

One of the things that attracts a lot of drivers to this gig is its entrepreneurial nature. You get to be your own boss and see a correlation between how hard you work and how much money you make. So it isn't surprising that many drivers have side hustles in addition to being a rideshare driver.

You are free to promote your side hustle, but it's important that you do it respectfully so as not to hurt your rating and so that your passengers might actually listen to what you have to say. Below are a few examples of how some drivers have accomplished this:

Peter - Do Your Park

Peter Vandendriesse started driving part-time for Uber and Lyft all the way back in 2014 in addition to his full-time job as an art director. He's also an entrepreneur, having founded a company called Do Your Park that aims to call out bad parking jobs by allowing customers to slap a small "you suck at parking" citation on the cars of bad parkers. Each magnet is reusable and displays a witty saying and illustration. Peter uses trivia with his rideshare passengers and passes out a single magnet if they're able to answer his questions correctly. That way, instead of him pushing his products on passengers, it feels more like a reward!

Janet - A Licensed Massage Therapist from Portland

Janet is a full-time licensed massage therapist, but when business is slow, she drives for Uber. A lot of passengers end up asking her what else she does, and at that point, it's pretty easy for her to talk about her other business. During Christmastime, she likes to offer gift certificates for her massage specials.

Speaking of side hustling, *New York Times* bestselling author Chris Guillebeau says that you should focus on what makes you special as a driver. He recommends drivers think like entrepreneurs if they want to break out beyond rideshare driving. Chris also says you should have a backup plan in case your first entrepreneurial endeavor fails—you don't have to tell anyone about your backup plan, but make sure to have one.

Listen to our interview with Chris on the podcast at therideshareguy.com/episode42.

10

What does the future look like for rideshare drivers?

A LOT GOES INTO BEING a rideshare driver, and if you've made it all the way to the end of this book, you're going to be better prepared than most.

Most drivers aren't prepared. They jump straight into this line of work without doing much research. One of the reasons they're able to do so is because it is an attractive job with relatively few barriers to entry.

The low barrier, while great when getting started, means a lot of drivers will flip on the app whenever they feel like it without thinking much about strategy. As we now know, you're responsible for your own success in this business and it's easy to make less than minimum wage without a strategic approach. You know better, but most new drivers don't; this creates problems in this industry that you should be aware of and may affect you as you build your rideshare business.

At the same time, this is a constantly evolving industry, meaning new services and companies are popping up that you will want to keep an eye on.

There's a lot of turnover with Uber and Lyft drivers

Uber has always had a big problem with retention and they've reported that half of all drivers quit after just one year.[32] How does that compare to other industries? One study by the Hay Group in 2012[33] found that retailers reported a median turnover rate of 67 percent for part-time workers. That number may seem high but it also makes a lot of sense. Many retail jobs are seasonal and/or temporary and I'm pretty sure most people don't grow up thinking they're going to work on an hourly basis at Hot Topic forever.

A lot of people feel the same way about driving for Uber. Although there are drivers who do it full-time, a majority of Uber drivers work less than ten hours per week. And Uber itself often touts flexibility as the number one reason why drivers drive for Uber. There's obviously less flexibility the more you have to drive, so it would make sense that Uber is best suited for part-time drivers.

In short, a lot of drivers hope to do this temporarily until they find something better, or they value the flexibility that

---

32   http://www.forbes.com/sites/briansolomon/2015/05/01/the-numbers-behind-ubers-exploding-driver-force/.

33   http://www.haygroup.com/us/press/details.aspx?id=33807.

allows them to pursue their passion (artists, actors, musicians, etc.).

Obviously, retail isn't the perfect comparison to driving for Uber since more attention goes into driving passengers than in retail, but it's close. One big difference between traditional retailers and Uber is that Uber doesn't spend much on training its drivers. Uber does pay big money for acquisition of drivers (paid marketing, sign-up bonuses, etc.) but once they have them, their on-boarding costs are minimal. Drivers don't have to meet anyone from the company face-to-face, and all the company really has to pay for is a background check.

One of the biggest complaints I hear from new drivers these days is that Uber doesn't pay enough. Uber has always seemed to put a premium on hiring new drivers over retaining existing drivers. After a series of huge corporate scandals though in early 2017, the tides appear to be changing and Uber is putting much more emphasis on improving the driver experience.

Uber and Lyft have always used investor money to pay big bonuses to new drivers and haven't had to worry about retention. But as the companies mature, they'll have to figure out some ways to improve the driver experience and maintain better driver retention rates. How can they do it?

Over the years, I've talked to tens of thousands of drivers and I've identified some of the top reasons why drivers are quitting. Uber and Lyft are starting to address some of these issues, but it's really a process of continuous improvement:

- **Low Pay:** From 2013–2016, Uber cut rates by 30 to 50 percent, which forced a lot of older and more experienced drivers to look for other opportunities (just ask your next few Uber drivers how long they've been driving). This is probably the number one complaint I hear from new drivers.

- **Driver Saturation and Less Surge:** Although Uber has constantly grown its passenger base, it seems like there are more drivers than ever on the roads. This is especially pronounced during big events like Halloween and New Year's Eve, which aren't nearly as profitable as they used to be. I suspect there are a lot more "weekend warriors" who only come out when it's busy. And innovations like UberPool mean fewer available rides for drivers.
- **Feeling Expendable:** Although Uber is getting better at this, it still doesn't feel like they value highly rated and experienced drivers. In the past, they would often take the customer's side in disputes and although they like to call their drivers "partners," it felt a lot more transactional than that. Lyft has done a better job with the driver community over the years and they have garnered a lot of loyal drivers because of it.
- **Inadequate Support:** One of the things I hear over and over from new drivers is that they feel like they're alone when they're getting started. Unlike a regular job, there are no coworkers that drivers can ask questions to or to help figure out how to do this or that. Drivers are left to figure things out for themselves. Uber's support system is getting better but can still be pretty frustrating at times.

Today, Uber and Lyft have a combined workforce of over a million drivers in the United States, but if you think about the sheer number of workers in similar industries like retail, you start to realize how many people could one day drive for rideshare services. In 2014, there were 77 million hourly workers,[34] of which 3 million were paid at or below the federal minimum wage of $7.25.

I estimate the earning potential of an Uber and Lyft driver to be $15–$20 per hour minus expenses, so imagine the number of people who would probably be better off financially by driving rideshare. Not to mention the fact that they'd also have some flexibility with the hours they worked.

Numbers and stats like this make me think that Uber and Lyft won't ever run out of drivers, but I do think they could face an even bigger problem. Uber and Lyft have built a ton of goodwill with customers since they provide a superior product. But as the best drivers leave for greener pastures, will they be able to maintain that quality?

Uber and Lyft provide very little in the way of training, and as they continue to look deeper and deeper into the workforce, the quality of their product could suffer if they don't continually look to improve.

Worries about self-driving cars

Rideshare companies' biggest expense right now are drivers, and self-driving cars present an opportunity for companies like Uber and Lyft to slash one of their biggest operating costs. Self-driving cars don't need breaks, they don't

---

34   http://www.bls.gov/opub/reports/cps/highlights-of-womens-earnings-in-2014.pdf.

complain, and since they'll be all electric, the maintenance costs will be much lower than traditional gas vehicles.

If you've ever ridden in a Tesla, you know that self-driving technology is already here. But I don't think rideshare drivers are going to be completely replaced any time soon. It's true that Uber, Lyft, and many other technology companies are investing billions of dollars in self-driving technology, but I think rideshare drivers will always be a part of the equation.

Companies like Uber and Lyft will likely spend the next ten to twenty years navigating the technological, political, and societal hurdles to overcome, but those problems will eventually be solved. But since self-driving cars are going to be so much cheaper to own and operate (since there's no driver), that's going to increase demand and make more people ditch their cars in favor of rideshare.

Since self-driving cars won't be able to fill all the demand, it's likely that there will be a hybrid fleet of self-driving cars and human drivers for some time to come. Uber and Lyft have also always leveraged the fact that they don't own any assets and rely on drivers to provide cars for their platform. This allows them to scale up quickly on Saturday nights when demand is at its highest but not have idle cars sitting around on Tuesday afternoons when demand is at its lowest.

Self-driving car fleet owners will face the same utilization problem, and peak times of demand may be another time where human drivers will still provide value. While self-driving technology is on the horizon, I don't ever envision a day where human drivers are completely out of the equation. So while it's good to be aware of it, for now, I wouldn't let it factor into your decision-making process.

Other rideshare companies to keep an eye on

Most people stick to driving for Uber and Lyft, but if you're looking to expand your repertoire, there's no shortage of companies to work for. Most of the smaller rideshare competitors operate on a local basis, but they can be a great addition since they often pay more and treat their workers better.

Juno (Gett)

Juno is only operating in New York and was recently acquired by Gett, but the new company is still operating under the Juno brand name, and for good reason. Juno burst onto the scene in 2016 with a driver-friendly model and gained a ton of goodwill among drivers. Although Uber is starting to catch up with some of the features Juno introduced like tipping and a 24/7 phone support line, the company is still popular with drivers in New York because of lower commissions and a driver-first focus.

Via

Via is a carpooling-only service based in New York City and Chicago that uses suburban-sized SUVs to ferry passengers around. They're growing quickly and we've heard good things from drivers who are working for them.

Fasten

Fasten is currently operating in Boston and Austin. Their app is very similar to the Uber experience but they take a much lower commission.

Wingz

Wingz focuses on prescheduled trips and has built a nice

niche in the airport pick-up and drop-off space since this is during a time where on-demand rides (like with Uber) aren't nearly as convenient.

Hop Skip Drive

Hop Skip Drive is based out of Southern California and focuses on rides exclusively for kids and teens. Their drivers have to have child care experience and go through in-person interviews in order to provide an extra layer of security.

Adding food and/or package delivery services

If you're looking for ultimate diversification, food and package delivery could be a great option for you. Typically, these delivery services don't pay as much on average as rideshare driving, but they also have more lenient requirements since you're not interacting in the same way with your customers.

Most delivery services only require their couriers to be eighteen years of age or older (versus twenty-one with rideshare) and there are no vehicle requirements. As long as your car runs, you can deliver! In some cities, you can even deliver on scooter, bicycle, or by foot.

> Some people do very well making deliveries via bicycle and like not having to deal with any gas costs! The Financial Panther is a blogger who side hustles as a Postmates courier using his bike, and he loves the ability to earn extra money and get some exercise at the same time.

As he notes, "being able to bring in around $200 per month from biking around town and getting exercise isn't so bad. It's way better than paying to go to the gym. From an hourly wage standpoint, I'd say I bring in around $12 to $15 per hour. It's not a lot of money. But if you're already planning to exercise, then this is just a way to get a bit of extra money from your exercise time."

You can read more about his experience delivering food on a bike at therideshareguy.com/FinancialPanther.

A lot of UberX drivers also do UberEATS since it's so easy to sign up if you're already an Uber driver, but a whole host of other food and grocery delivery companies are out there: DoorDash, Postmates, Caviar, GrubHub and Instacart.

As you can see, there are quite a few options but first you'll want to check whether these services are available in your city. Food delivery isn't as widespread as rideshare so if you're in a smaller city, you may not be able to deliver just yet. But at their core, the pay and the job is pretty similar across most of these services.

Customers will place an order, and at partner restaurants, all you'll need to do is go in and find your order, pick up the food and deliver it. At non-partner restaurants like fast-food joints, you'll need to physically place the order, wait for the food, and deliver it.

Typically, a little more logistical work is involved with delivery since you may have to place an order, confirm the correct food is there, and keep the customer apprised of the situation (possible delays for example). But there's also less interaction with the actual customer, so for some drivers, that's a nice change of pace since you can listen to your own music for once!

One of the reasons why I personally like delivering food is because the peak times of demand for food delivery line up well with the slow times for rideshare. During the week, rideshare is really busy during commuting hours but slow during the middle of the day. As you might imagine, food delivery is busiest during weekdays at lunch when everyone is ordering food.

If you're really looking to maximize your income, below is what the optimal eight hour day could look like:

07:00 a.m.–10:00 a.m.: Rideshare Morning Rush (three hours)
10:00 a.m.–11:30 a.m.: Mid-morning break
11:30 a.m.–01:30 p.m.: Delivery Lunch-time Rush (two hours)
01:30 p.m.–04:30 p.m.: Mid-afternoon break
03:30 p.m.–06:30 p.m.: Rideshare Afternoon Rush (three hours)

Obviously everyone's schedule will be a little different, but you'll want to experiment and find times of maximum demand for rideshare and for delivery and see where they line up with your schedule. If you are an early riser, you might shift your schedule up a few hours and do all the early a.m. airport runs from 5 to 7 a.m.

Delivering for Amazon Flex

One of the most popular package delivery services is Amazon Flex. This gig involves delivering Prime Now packages and groceries. Amazon Flex is shift-based so drivers typically earn $17+/hour, but you have to deliver all of your packages if you want to be paid.

Amazon Flex is expanding rapidly and they often pay higher rates when they first launch, but one of the downsides to working for them is shift availability. Unlike Uber and Lyft where you can go online whenever you want, with Flex you'll need to book shifts in advance, which be quite competitive.

Conclusion

When I first started driving for Uber and Lyft, I would never have imagined that so much could go into driving people around for money. Uber and Lyft don't provide a ton of training, so you have a lot of new drivers who feel like they're on their own, but you're not alone!

All of the concepts in this book may seem like a lot to digest at first, but over time, they become second nature. A savvy driver knows that there are no guarantees when it comes to rideshare driving and it pays to be strategic—and sometimes even a little cutthroat.

And like anything in life, there are positives and negatives to this job. You will have some expenses, liability, and reporting requirements to worry about, but those can be mitigated with smart planning and preparation. We've even shared tools that will help automate this process and allow you to focus on the fun part: earning more money. For me, the positives clearly outweigh the negatives and I love being able to take advantage of the flexibility and earning potential of rideshare driving.

Not everyone will be able to make this gig work, but I'm confident that this book will give you the best chance for success. It's important to do your due diligence and research, but ultimately it will be up to you to execute and apply what you've learned.

So don't forget to work smarter, not harder, and drive safe out there!

—Harry, "The Rideshare Guy"

Appendix

Abbreviations

ETA - Estimated Time to Arrival

NYC - New York City

QBSE - Quickbooks Self-Employed

TCP - Transportation Charter Permit

TNC - Transportation Network Company

TLC - Taxi & Limousine Commission

Links

www.therideshareguy.com/newuberdriver

www.therideshareguy.com/newlyftdriver

www.therideshareguy.com/sign-up-bonuses

www.therideshareguy.com/phonemounts

www.therideshareguy.com/dashcams

www.therideshareguy.com/qbse

www.therideshareguy.com/stridedrive

www.therideshareguy.com/insurance

www.therideshareguy.com/mystro

therideshareguy.com/uberinquiry

help.Uber.com

twitter.com/Uber_support

facebook.com/Uber/

therideshareguy.com/facebookgroups

reddit.com/r/uberdrivers

reddit.com/r/lyftdrivers

UberPeople.net

TheRideshareGuy.com

RidesharingDriver.com

RideshareApps.com

therideshareguy.com/UberMan

therideshareguy.com/thesimpledriver

therideshareguy.com/Jermaine

therideshareguy.com/rideshareprofessor

therideshareguy.com/itunes

therideshareguy.com/mileageapps

therideshareguy.com/palm1

therideshareguy.com/CPM

therideshareguy.com/episode42

therideshareguy.com/episode57

therideshareguy.com/episode37

therideshareguy.com/episode43

therideshareguy.com/episode4

therideshareguy.com/episode17

therideshareguy.com/FinancialPanther

therideshareguy.com/JayCradeur

therideshareguy.com/Vehicles

therideshareguy.com/passenger/uber

therideshareguy.com/passenger/lyft

Index

About the
Author

Harry Campbell started driving for Uber and Lyft in his spare time back in 2014 while he was working as an aerospace engineer for Boeing. Harry quickly latched on to ridesharing, but he also noticed that there was a void of information out there and many drivers were struggling with the basics of getting started, signing up, and maximizing their income.

In 2014, Harry started blogging about his experience as a driver on The Rideshare Guy. Eventually, he quit his job as an engineer to focus on the blog full-time. Today, The Rideshare Guy is one of the leading authorities regarding driver-focused content on the web. The blog, YouTube channel, podcast, and video training course reach hundreds of thousands of drivers every single month. Harry is also a trusted media source, having been featured in top publications such as *The New York Times*, *Bloomberg*, *WIRED*, and CNN.

You can learn more about Harry and see what he's up to on TheRideshareGuy.com.